POLICY ANALYSES IN INTERNATIONAL ECONOMICS **37**

TRADE AND PAYMENTS AFTER SOVIET DISINTEGRATION

John Williamson

INSTITUTE FOR INTERNATIONAL ECONOMICS
WASHINGTON, DC
June 1992

John Williamson, Senior Fellow at the Institute, was economics professor at Pontifícia Universidade Católica do Rio de Janeiro (1978–81), University of Warwick (1970–77), Massachusetts Institute of Technology (1967, 1980), University of York (1963–68), and Princeton University (1962–63); Advisor to the International Monetary Fund (1972–74); and Economic Consultant to the UK Treasury (1968–70). He has published numerous studies on international monetary issues, Third World debt and other topics, including *From Soviet disUnion to Eastern Economic Community?* (1991), *Currency Convertibility in Eastern Europe* (1991), *Latin American Adjustment: How Much Has Happened?* (1990), and *Targets and Indicators: A Blueprint for the International Coordination of Economic Policy* (1987).

INSTITUTE FOR INTERNATIONAL ECONOMICS
11 Dupont Circle, NW
Washington, DC 20036-1207
(202) 328-9000   FAX: (202) 328-5432

C. Fred Bergsten, *Director*
Linda Griffin Kean, *Director of Publications*

The views expressed in this publication are those of the author. This publication is part of the overall program of the Institute, as endorsed by its Board of Directors, but does not necessarily reflect the views of individual members of the Board or the Advisory Committee.

Printed in the United States of America   94 93 92 91   3 2 1

Library of Congress Cataloging-in-Publication Data

Williamson, John, 1937–
    Trade and payments after Soviet disintegration / John Williamson.
        p. cm.—(Policy analyses in international economics; 37)
    "July 1992."
    Includes bibliographical references and index.
    ISBN 0-88132-173-7
    1. Former Soviet republics—Commercial policy—Congresses.
2. Debts, External—Former Soviet republics—Congresses. I. Title.
II. Series.
HF1557.W55   1992   92-21821
382.3'0947—dc20   CIP

Contents

TABLES

Preface

Economic reform in the former Soviet Union will remain one of the most critical world economic issues for the foreseeable future. Its impact is likely to range far beyond economics, affecting both the prospects for democratization in the newly independent republics and the future global security situation. There will also be a considerable impact on relations among the United States and the other industrial democracies as they seek a common view on how best to support the reforms, and how to share the costs of doing so.

One key set of questions posed by the Soviet breakup concerns the future economic relationships among Russia and the other republics. All the republics were linked so intimately during the Communist period that, even if they do everything right internally, a collapse of interrepublic trade could still doom their economic prospects. Any policy package that seeks to promote successful reform in the former Soviet Union, and thus any program of external assistance, must address this issue effectively.

The Institute, foreseeing the disintegration of the Soviet economy, launched in early 1991 the project that produced this study. Some early results were released in October 1991 in a study coauthored by Oleh Havrylyshyn and John Williamson under the title *From Soviet disUnion to Eastern Economic Community?* Further intensive analysis was carried out in collaboration with three leading Russian economists (including Andrey Vavilov, who subsequently became First Deputy Finance Minister to Yegor Gaidar) in residence at the Institute. The project culminated with a major conference in Vienna in April 1992, organized jointly by the Institute and the Austrian National Bank in association with the Russian League of Industrialists and Entrepreneurs. This study draws heavily on the papers and discussion at that conference but reflects the personal conclusions of John Williamson rather than a consensus of the group.

As we have done on a number of occasions, the Institute is releasing the results of this project in two different forms to meet the needs of different audiences. The present study presents, as indicated, John Williamson's own analysis and appraisal of the problem and possible solutions. We will shortly publish a conference volume from the Vienna meeting that will include all of the papers presented there, some of which suggest alternative approaches. That volume will also include detailed studies of each of the republics of the former Soviet Union and the implications for them of the breakup of the previous single economy.

The Institute for International Economics is a private nonprofit institution for the study and discussion of international economic policy. Its purpose is to analyze important issues in that area, and to develop and communicate practical new approaches for dealing with them. The Institute is completely nonpartisan.

The Institute is funded largely by philanthropic foundations. Major institutional grants are now being received from the German Marshall Fund of the United States, which created the Institute with a generous commitment of funds in 1981, and from the Ford Foundation, the William and Flora Hewlett Foundation, the William M. Keck, Jr. Foundation, the Alfred P. Sloan Foundation, the C. V. Starr Foundation, and the United States-Japan Foundation. A number of other foundations and private corporations also contribute to the highly diversified financial resources of the Institute. About 14 percent of the Institute's resources in our latest fiscal year were provided by contributors outside the United States, including about 6 percent from Japan. The Austrian National Bank hosted and funded the Vienna conference in April 1992 on which much of this study is based.

The Board of Directors bears overall responsibility for the Institute and gives general guidance and approval to its research program—including identification of topics that are likely to become important to international economic policymakers over the medium run (generally, one to three years), and which thus should be addressed by the Institute. The Director, working closely with the staff and outside Advisory Committee, is responsible for the development of particular projects and makes the final decision to publish an individual study.

The Institute hopes that its studies and other activities will contribute to building a stronger foundation for international economic policy around the world. We invite readers of these publications to let us know how they think we can best accomplish this objective.

C. FRED BERGSTEN
Director
June 1992

Acknowledgments

The author acknowledges with gratitude the stimulus provided by the authors, discussants, panelists, and floor participants at the conference cosponsored by the Institute and the Austrian National Bank in Vienna on 20–22 April 1992. Helpful comments on an earlier draft were received from Sergey Alexashenko, C. Fred Bergsten, Peter Knight, Michael Marrese, Kent Osband, and the participants in a seminar at the Vienna Institute for Comparative Economic Studies in June 1992.

1 Introduction

The successor states of the Soviet Union are seeking what are surely the most dramatic social transformations in human history. Almost all of them are aiming to build functioning democracies, in an area with practically no democratic traditions on which to draw. All have declared their intention of moving to a market economy, despite there being even less memory of the market than in the Central European countries that pioneered the transition. And, as if that were not enough, the 15 former Soviet republics are trying to build new independent states on the rubble of the last of the world's great multinational empires.

This study concerns the interactions between the second and third of these ambitions: between the aim to transform these economies to a market basis and the replacement of a centralized empire by a series of nation-states. Will market-determined trade between independent states continue with the same intensity, and in the same direction, as that inherited from the Soviet Union? Is there a danger of this trade collapsing, and how severe would the consequences of such a collapse be? What policy measures might avert the danger of a collapse in trade, while helping to shift it to a market basis? How much interest do the new states have in maintaining cooperative relationships among themselves, and what institutional forms might cooperation take?

In association with Oleh Havrylyshyn, the author took a preliminary look at this range of questions shortly after it became clear that the Soviet Union was in the process of disintegrating (Havrylyshyn and Williamson 1991). We were at that time already planning to hold a conference on the subject in the course of the following year. That conference was held in Vienna in April 1992, convened jointly by the Institute for International Economics and the Austrian National Bank, in association with the Russian League of Industrialists and Entrepreneurs. The present study is based on that conference. The subject matter is in such a state of chaos that it would be surprising if the questions were answered as satisfactorily as one might wish, but it is

1

hoped that both the forthcoming conference volume (Williamson 1992b) and this summary and synthesis of the conference will nonetheless make a constructive contribution to analysis of the policy options in the Commonwealth of Independent States (CIS) as well as in the West.

The study starts by outlining the difficult inheritance left by the Soviet Union to all of the new states. It proceeds to an analysis of the range of economic problems created by the dissolution of the Soviet Union. The next section lays out the options on the most contentious of the issues at stake, namely, the choice of a payments system to finance intratrade among the successor states. The penultimate section develops policy recommendations, and the concluding remarks summarize the implied answers to the set of questions laid out above. An appendix sketches the position of each of the republics.

2 The Inheritance

Six years of perestroika destroyed not just the traditional command economy of the Soviet Union, but also the "bargaining economy" that some analysts argued had replaced the command economy as the center progressively lost its power to dictate to the enterprises. Two of the conference papers, those by Sergey Alexashenko and Evgeni Yasin, argue persuasively that the damage was done primarily by the fiscal deficit, which increased from an easily financeable 2.4 percent of GDP in 1985 to close to 10 percent in 1987–90 and more than 20 percent in 1991. In an economy with no mechanism for financing budget deficits other than the printing press, this led to a monetary explosion. The combination of budget deficit, monetary explosion, and universal price controls generated excess demand, massive payments deficits, a large monetary overhang, and a progressive disappearance of goods from the shelves at official prices.

More and more goods came to be sold at unregulated prices, both consumer goods on the free markets and intermediate goods on the new commercial exchanges. The supply system was nonetheless disrupted, in part by excess demand (the unavailability of critical inputs), to the point where output fell by over 2 percent in 1990 and 15 percent in 1991. Capital flight developed, primarily because rubles could not be used to buy anything internally. By late 1991 the Soviet Union was unable to service its external debt and was obliged to ask the Group of Seven (G-7) countries for a moratorium.

The Soviet Union under Mikhail Gorbachev's leadership (1985–91) did achieve progress in some dimensions. Most of these were political: glasnost, elections, respect for human rights, and the ending of the Cold War were massive achievements by any standard. Even in the economic realm some of the seeds of reform were sown: enterprises did achieve independence from the central planners (although by August 1991 they had still not started to make much constructive use of it), the beginnings of a private sector emerged in the cooperative movement and individual entrepreneurship, and a two-tier banking system was established (but not adequately regulated or capitalized).

The situation of the Soviet economy in its final months was bleak. Inflation was largely repressed by price controls, to the point where almost nothing except a few spices was freely available at the official prices in Moscow, yet prices were still rising by several percent each month. A dollar was valued at 1.6 rubles according to the "commercial" exchange rate at which enterprises were supposed to surrender most of their foreign-exchange earnings,[1] yet a foreigner could buy around 100 rubles for a dollar on the parallel market. Public services were progressively deteriorating. Corruption was rampant and confidence nonexistent.

The collapse had not gone as far in some of the other republics as it had in Russia, so many of them did not feel under the same pressure to embark on an immediate program of price liberalization. Add to that the free-rider problem created by a common currency in the presence of independent fiscal policies, which meant that each of the smaller states perceived that its own deficit spending would not have a significant impact on the level of monetary emission and hence on inflation, and one can understand why the other republics did not all share the Russian sense of urgency in pushing ahead with reform.

When the Soviet Union vanished in December 1991 and its former republics declared themselves independent nations, none except Russia—which was able to take over most of the Soviet institutions—had the basic institutional infrastructure needed to run a modern state. All the republics had branches of the former ministries which they proceeded to convert into full-fledged ministries. In some cases, for example the branches of Gosplan (the planning ministry) and of the industry ministries, the well-wishers of a market economy might actually have desired that these institutions be less able to continue functioning autonomously. However, in the key economic ministries like finance there were acute problems of inexperience and a shortage of trained

---

1. There was also an even more ludicrously overvalued "official" exchange rate of 0.6 ruble to the dollar, but no transactions took place at that rate.

personnel (for example, Kyrghyzstan is reported to have a Ministry of Finance with a staff of a dozen). The same was true of the branches of Gosbank (the Soviet central bank), which became republic central banks, but without any of the traditions of central banking or employees familiar with such basic matters as how to print money, let alone how to conduct a monetary policy.

Even Russia had problems, including the lack of a customs service on its new borders with the other republics. Insofar as this impeded the erection of trade barriers among the republics, this was not without its advantages. But given that energy and many raw materials were priced internally far below their world prices at any realistic exchange rate, Russia was greatly concerned about the possibility of primary commodities being reexported through other republics, which would then capture much of the rents.

There were also problems of dividing the assets and, more important, the liabilities of the old Soviet Union among the new states. The G-7 insisted that the foreign debt be divided among the states but then be guaranteed by them "jointly and severally"—in other words, each of them would hold itself legally responsible for the whole debt. Since it is ridiculous to think that Armenia (say) could in any meaningful sense be held responsible for a Russian failure to service its portion of the debt, this language was presumably intended to be a formula either for getting Russia to take responsibility for the whole of the debt, or for bolstering Russian hegemony. Ukraine and Uzbekistan seem to have adopted the latter interpretation, for it was they rather than Russia that balked at the formula.

Difficult as these economic questions were, they were dwarfed by the political disputes revealed by Soviet disintegration. The overblown armed forces had to be divided up, and to satisfy the West that had to be done without increasing the number of nuclear powers in the world, while also assuaging the desire of all the states that had inherited nuclear weapons to keep some element of control over their use. Borders had in many cases been drawn quite casually, as when Nikita Khrushchev gave the Crimea to Ukraine as a present in the 1950s, on the assumption that these borders really did not matter much since the whole empire was administered from the center. Partly as a result, there are large ethnic minorities in all of the republics, including some 25 million Russians living outside Russia and a comparable number of non-Russians living within Russia. Considering the potential for disaster and some of the historical precedents of decolonization, it is right to recognize that the dismemberment of the Russian empire has so far been accomplished in a relatively civilized way. The crucial question to be discussed in this study is whether it can also be achieved without causing an economic catastrophe.

3 The Problems Posed by Disintegration

Despite its formal federal structure, the Soviet Union operated as a highly centralized state. It is therefore not surprising to find that its collapse has confronted the successor states with severe problems. The present section outlines six critical problems that will need to be resolved in designing arrangements for trade and payments of, and among, the newly independent republics in a post-Soviet world.

The Need for New Trade Patterns

Soviet planners had a very clear idea of the sort of trade patterns they wished to see. The Soviet Union, or at least the area of the Council for Mutual Economic Assistance (CMEA, which also included the Central European countries), should be self-sufficient, but each of its component parts should act as a branch of a giant factory.[1] Hence the pattern of very low levels of exports to the outside world, even including the other CMEA members, combined with very high levels of trade among the republics.

This "socialist division of labor" was pushed to an extreme. One of the unfortunate legacies, detailed in the conference paper by Tim Snyder, is the extraordinarily high degree of monopoly in the former Soviet republics. Since the planners regarded competition as a social waste rather than the stimulus that makes an economy efficient and motivates innovation, they were unconcerned by the prevalence of monopoly. Indeed, since they also underpriced transportation and had an exaggerated faith in economies of scale, they tended to regard public monopolies as rational and beneficent institutions.

---

1. In his conference comment, Dmitri Subbotin suggested that their purpose was less to create a single factory than to create a single military fortress, which led the planners to duplicate many productive facilities with a view to ensuring that at least one would survive in a military conflict.

A conference paper by Oleg Vjugin and Andrey Vavilov attempted to project how the pattern of trade would change in the long run assuming that market economies are established in the former Soviet republics. They used a gravity model (in which trade flows are estimated *inter alia* as an inverse function of distance) calibrated on 19 industrial countries (15 European countries plus the United States, Canada, Japan, and Korea) to estimate what the volume and direction of trade of each of the new states will be after they have adjusted and become integrated into the world economy—a process that one would expect to take a decade or more.

The results of the model led Vjugin and Vavilov to conclude that the absolute level of trade of the former Soviet republics will decline in the long run.[2] That is, market forces can be expected to motivate efficient net import substitution, so that goods currently produced in only a few locations in the former Soviet Union and then sold to the other states will be produced in a larger number of states. Note that this does not imply that the economies of the republics will be more "closed" than in the past: as Evgeni Yasin argued in his conference paper,[3] an open economy is one that responds to events abroad, not one that swaps large quantities of goods with foreign countries regardless of circumstances.

The model yielded a second and equally striking conclusion: that there will be a dramatic shift in the direction of trade, away from intratrade among the former republics and toward the rest of the world. For example, the model suggested that, in a full disintegration scenario, Russia could be expected to send only some 13 percent of its exports to the other ex-Soviet republics, as opposed to the 57 percent of its exports that it sent there in 1987. Similarly, the proportion of Ukrainian exports destined for the other republics would drop from 80 percent to under 20 percent, those of Belarus from 84 percent to 23 percent, and the remaining republics would experience declines from over 85 percent to something under 20 percent.

---

2. However, several conference participants argued that gravity models are subject to large errors in predicting the volume—as opposed to the direction—of trade.

3. ". . . the Soviet economy because of its planned nature was a closed economy, irrespective of the level of external trade."

Although the extent of the projected decline in intratrade is surprising, these conclusions are not a freak. They parallel those of Collins and Rodrik (1991), who also detected, using a different method, a probable future reorientation of the trade of the countries of Eastern Europe away from the former CMEA area and toward the West. They were also checked by Vjugin and Vavilov in two ways: by using a second group of countries, located in the Middle East and Asia, in order to calibrate the gravity model; and by comparing the results of the gravity model with calculations that used the Collins and Rodrik methodology insofar as this was possible. Finally, another gravity model has been estimated, by Gros and Dautrebande (1992), and yielded broadly similar results. Thus one may expect that a successful transition to market economies combined with outward-oriented economic policies will ultimately induce a *reduction* in the total volume of trade and a substantial redirection of trade away from intratrade and toward the rest of the world. Intratrade may settle at no more than some 20 percent to 30 percent of its level of 1987.

Vjugin and Vavilov examined the potential impact of a free trade agreement in modifying the predicted reduction in intratrade. They used a dummy variable to estimate the impact of the European Community and the European Free Trade Association (EFTA) in stimulating intra-European trade, and then introduced the same dummy into their gravity model. They concluded that a free trade arrangement would increase the share of intratrade by some 4 to 7 percentage points: for example, Russian exports to the other former Soviet republics would be some 17 percent of total Russian exports rather than 13 percent, those of Ukraine would be some 24 percent instead of 18 percent, and so on. The differences are noticeable, but most of the projected shift in the pattern of trade would still materialize. Thus, the projected redirection of trade is not so much a consequence of the disappearance of a common economic space as of the move to a market economy and the opening of borders.

The Need for New Trade Mechanisms

The shift to a market economy will require a fundamental change in the way in which trade is conducted, away from the sort of interstate barter agreements that were negotiated in 1991 and toward direct contracts between enterprises.

As the republics gained more and more power in the course of 1990–91, they began to sign what were called barter agreements in an attempt to prevent a breakdown of interrepublic trade. The government of one republic would commit itself to supplying a long list of goods to another republic, in return for which it was promised another long list of goods. Payment was to be made in rubles.

The classic disadvantage of barter—the fact that it precludes efficient triangular trade and instead relies on a double coincidence of wants— is the least of the disadvantages of this arrangement. A more important drawback, which became apparent very quickly, is that it contained inadequate incentives for the sellers to fulfill the terms of the agreements. Where goods were in short supply at the controlled prices that prevailed, it made more sense for republics to keep the goods at home than to ship them off in fulfillment of a barter agreement, in the knowledge that all they would receive in exchange might be rubles (which could be obtained much more cheaply at home by the republic central bank creating more credit). This led not just to a growth of export restrictions, but also to failures to fulfill the terms of the barter agreements that republics had signed—failures that provoked strong complaints in several of the conference papers, most notably Beisenbay Izteleuov's paper on Kazakhstan.

A second problem with the barter agreements is that they are poorly specified. In some cases obligations are designated in physical terms, for example as so many tons of oil or so many kilowatt-hours of electricity to be supplied in the course of a year, but even then a failure to specify delivery dates or the time of day when the electricity is to be transmitted creates endless opportunities for disagreement and/or unintended disruption of supply in the importing state. In other cases the obligation is specified in terms of a given ruble value of some good (like furs) to be shipped, which in an environment of near-hyperinflation obviously invites delays in shipping the goods.

The most fundamental difficulty with these barter agreements, however, is that they require the state to do what it is supposedly in the process of renouncing: issue state orders so as to procure the goods that can then be supplied in fulfillment of the obligation enshrined in the barter agreement. This difficulty cannot be finessed by raising prices to market-clearing levels or by more careful drafting of the agreements.

If the members of the CIS are serious about creating a market economy, they must abandon interstate barter agreements formally and move to enterprise-to-enterprise trade. The commodity exchanges that have emerged from the grassroots over the last two years now provide a mechanism for negotiating such contracts.

In fact, the barter agreements seem to be functioning more like clearing agreements, with indicative lists of products that will be accepted up to certain limits, than as hard commitments to supply specified quantities. Prices are often left open to negotiation. This is at least a move toward enterprise-to -enterprise trade.

Much of such trade as does take place between enterprises at the moment remains in the form of barter. This is primarily a consequence of the near-breakdown of the settlement mechanism. This problem is discussed at the beginning of section 4.

The Threat of a Trade Collapse

It is one thing to argue that in the long term intratrade should decrease. It is quite another to view with equanimity a precipitate collapse of that trade. As Yasin says in his paper, "However irrational [past links] may be, their overnight discontinuance would lead to the complete collapse of the economy." No one at the conference challenged the proposition that most of the very intensive trade among the republics that had been deliberately fostered by the central planners has to be maintained in the short run if the economies are not to be reduced to chaos. That trade can sensibly be allowed to run down only as new investment makes possible the redeployment of factors into alternative uses and the satisfaction of needs from alternative sources.

History shows the cost of arbitrarily disrupting existing trade channels. For example, the successor states of the Austro-Hungarian Empire other than Czechoslovakia all retrogressed or stagnated throughout the interwar period, in marked contrast to the Empire's record as the fourth fastest-growing economy in Europe prior to World War I. Most historians have argued that a major cause of the problem was the erection of trade barriers between the newly independent states.

Another case concerns Western Europe after World War II. Marshall Plan aid is widely credited with having accelerated recovery, yet in fact US aid was no greater after Marshall aid started to flow than before. The crucial difference was in the conditionality attached to the aid, which required Europeans to help themselves by dismantling the restrictions that had been blocking their mutual trade. What De Long and Eichengreen (1992) have characterized as "history's most successful structural adjustment program" required that the search for bilateral trade balance be abandoned. The revival of intra-European trade helped launch the European recovery.

As noted in the appendix, many of the conference papers asserted that intratrade has been severely reduced in 1992 and gave this as a significant cause of both declining output levels and falling standards of living. The evidence is fragmentary rather than statistically well documented, but it is nonetheless compelling. It seems that fears about the danger of a collapse of intratrade are being realized. This is presumably in part because of the inadequacies of barter agreements as discussed above. (Of course, the initial effect of making the needed move to enterprise-to-enterprise trade might prove to be further disruption: it will doubtless take time to work in the new system.)

In his conference paper, Alexander Granberg cited the results of models constructed in Novosibirsk that aimed to calculate the consequences of a severance of interrepublic trade. One of these shows that Russia, with the most diversified economy, has a "self-supply" coefficient of almost 65 percent, and gains less than 15 percent of its consumption from interrepublic interactions (the remainder being imputed to foreign trade). For other republics "self-supply" accounts for 44 percent, interrepublic trade for 39 percent, and foreign trade for 17 percent. The implication is that while all the republics, including Russia, gain from intratrade, its collapse would have far more severe consequences for the non-Russian republics.

A Western attempt to analyze the consequences of a severance of intratrade has been made by Nuti and Pisani-Ferry (1992), using Goskomstat data. These estimates are shown in table 1. They assume that republics could sell "hard goods" like energy, raw materials, and 50 percent of chemicals and food products on the world market if other republics ceased to buy from them, but that the loss of markets for "soft goods"—essentially finished manufactures and services—would

T A B L E 1 **Potential cost to individual republics of a disruption of trade links with the rest of the ruble zone**

Republic	Republic's loss[a]		Russia's loss[b]		Ratio of republic's loss to Russia's loss
	Billions of rubles	Percentages of NMP	Billions of rubles	Percentages of NMP	
Armenia	2,917	50.3	1,044	0.3	2.8
Azerbaijan	3,963	36.4	1,962	0.5	2.0
Belarus	13,869	52.9	4,716	1.2	2.9
Estonia	2,093	51.1	738	0.2	2.8
Georgia	3,665	35.9	1,836	0.5	2.0
Kazakhstan	3,359	12.5	4,842	1.3	0.7
Kyrghyzstan	1,914	38.3	900	0.2	2.1
Latvia	3,650	52.1	1,260	0.3	2.9
Lithuania	4,115	46.2	1,602	0.4	2.6
Moldova	3,467	45.0	1,386	0.4	2.5
Russia	44,168	11.5	NA	NA	NA
Tajikistan	1,519	31.7	864	0.2	1.8
Turkmenistan	1,327	28.2	846	0.2	1.6
Ukraine	24,775	24.2	18,448	4.8	1.3
Uzbekistan	5,515	26.6	3,726	1.0	1.5

NMP = net material product; NA = not applicable.

a. Republic's loss is measured by exports of "soft goods" (defined as finished manufacturers services, 50 percent of chemicals, and 50 percent of food products) to the rest of the ruble zone.

b. Russia's loss is measured by Russia's exports of "soft goods" to the state. Calculation assumes that exports are distributed according to the republics' NMPs.

Source: D. Mario Nuti and Jean Pisani-Ferry. 1992. "Post-Soviet Issues: Stabilization, Trade and Money." Paper presented at a conference on "The Economic Consequences of the East," Frankfurt (April), table 4. The authors used Goskomstat data for 1989.

result in a loss of output because these goods would be unsaleable elsewhere. These figures are, the authors acknowledge, upper bounds on the potential cost of the disruption of intratrade. The results, which are broadly parallel to those reported by Granberg, are nonetheless striking: they show that the total costs of a breakdown in trade would be very substantial indeed. Russia and Kazakhstan would suffer least (because the bulk of their exports to other republics consist of hard goods), whereas the cost to many of the small republics would be crippling (reaching a maximum of 53 percent of net material product [NMP] in the case of Belarus). This asymmetry in the costs of a trade collapse is one of the fundamental facts that the smaller republics have to take into account before giving vent to dissatisfaction with Russian hegemonic behavior.

It became very clear in the course of the Vienna conference that the CIS is not providing an effective mechanism for defusing the tensions inherent in the relations between Russia and the smaller republics. It is often argued that the commonwealth was set up to facilitate the final dismantling of the Soviet state, rather than to provide a framework for long-term economic cooperation on the model of the European Community. The organization has no funds and no staff. If multilateral economic cooperation among the members of the CIS is to be revived, the CIS needs either to be reformed or to be replaced.

Monetary Control

One of the first and most disruptive consequences of the erosion of central authority in the Soviet Union was the progressive loss of monetary control. Under the *ancien régime* it did not matter very much that the central bank automatically monetized the deficits of the republic governments as well as the union government, because the union government kept its own deficit down and made sure that the republic governments did too. But the practice of automatic monetary emission was carried over to a situation where the union government was letting its own finances deteriorate and the republic governments were gaining a large measure of autonomy in their fiscal policy. Since most of the costs of monetary emission by any one republic spill over to the others under a common monetary system, while the benefits of the deficit spending accrue exclusively to the republic that runs a deficit, the system gave each individual republic an incentive to run a deficit even though the collective consequence was inevitably either repressed or open inflation.[4] In fact the situation was even worse in 1991, inasmuch

---

4. See the discussion in Havrylyshyn and Williamson (1991, 30–31).

as Russia, which as the largest republic had the clearest incentive not to act as a free rider, wielded its monetary power with a view to destabilizing the union government. The Soviet Union ended up with a budget deficit of around 20 percent of GDP in its final year of existence.

This problem was recognized very quickly by the Russian economic team appointed in November 1991 and headed by First Deputy Prime Minister Yegor Gaidar. That same month Gaidar's team moved to assert unilateral Russian control of the emission of cash rubles, indicating that other republics would be entitled to obtain ruble banknotes on a scale commensurate with Russian emission, but no larger. This evoked strong complaints from some of the other republics. Moreover, they now complain that Russia has not in fact delivered rubles on the same scale as they have been issued in Russia itself. An additional grievance is that Russia has been charging interest (admittedly only at the strongly negative real rate implied by a nominal interest rate of 22 percent per year) on the credit represented by "lending" the ruble banknotes to the other republics. In other words, Russia is refusing to share the seigniorage in ruble creation.

Ruble banknotes are not, however, the only problem. Even though the lack of banknotes constrained the governments of the other republics in their ability to finance budget deficits with the public, their central banks could still extend credit to their enterprises. The enterprises could use that credit *inter alia* to buy goods from Russia, implying that excess monetary emission in the other republics could still occur and might undermine Russia's stabilization program.

Sergei Vasiliev points out in his conference paper that Russia has made another major change:

> In January 1992, the Russian credit system began to switch over to correspondent-type relations between the republics' central banks and the Central Bank of Russia. This, in fact, meant a unilateral nationalization of the ruble. The plan, scheduled to be completed in the second half of 1992, will help the Central Bank of Russia to impose an effective ceiling on the growth of credit supply in other republics. For example, as soon as any republic prints money at a rate exceeding that in Russia, a limiting mechanism comes into action.
>
> This mechanism works as follows. A higher rate of credit growth . . . would send local prices soaring and . . . lead to increased Russian exports and a trade deficit [for the other republic]. Eventually the ballooning trade deficit will drain the republic's correspondent account with the Central

Bank of Russia, leaving the republic high and dry. As this republic's bank teeters toward insolvency, it comes to face a stark choice: Russian credits or bankruptcy. Should it choose the second option, the Central Bank of Russia immediately stops all payments from within the bankrupt republic. Cut off from the Russian clearance turnover, the clearance checks of this bank form the basis for a quasi-currency of this republic.

In fact the payments mechanism is not yet working exactly as this account would suggest. The old all-union settlement system allowed direct branch-to-branch interbank transfers. Under current (May 1992) procedures, the Central Bank of Russia is informed *ex post* when inter-republic payments are cleared, which is a lengthy process because the interbank settlement mechanism has almost broken down, and it then adds or subtracts the balance to each republic's account. The other central banks apparently do not know what their balances are on a running basis.

The significance of this change is nonetheless vastly greater than yet seems to have been appreciated in the West.[5] It means that, once the system is fully operational, enterprises in other republics will no longer be able to spend rubles in their bank accounts as though these were Russian rubles available to buy Russian goods in unlimited quantities. Instead, because such payments will be funneled through the accounts of a correspondent bank, Russia will be able to keep track of the balance of each state and can suspend exports to any state that runs an excessive cumulative import surplus and overdraws its correspondent account. This will give Russia a tool that it can use to avoid accepting bank-deposit rubles created in the other states.

It is important to understand that even before reform the Soviet Union had essentially two different monies: the cash ruble used by

---

5. Both the IMF studies of the ex-Soviet republics based on their membership negotiations (IMF 1992) and recent press analyses (such as Wolf 1992) continue to speak of the ruble as a common currency. Nuti and Pisani-Ferry (1992, 16) indicate awareness of the issue, but they choose to emphasize that "national central banks [in the other republics] seem to be able to extend unlimited ruble credit to their governments or . . . commercial banks . . . while Russia de facto validates this money creation by accepting payments in rubles from the other republics." Although Russia has not yet actually refused to validate such money creation, it is in a position to do so, or at least very close to such a position.

households and the bank-deposit ruble used by enterprises. The two were totally inconvertible into each other except when an enterprise wished to pay wages or to deposit the proceeds of sales to the public, at which time it drew or deposited (respectively) cash rubles at an exchange rate of 1:1. Perestroika created opportunities for the cooperatives to arbitrage between the two markets, as a result of which an exchange rate (of around 1.3 bank-deposit rubles for 1 cash ruble in early 1992) emerged between them. The requirement that interrepublic payments be channeled through correspondent accounts means that bank-deposit rubles will no longer be automatically exchangeable throughout the former Soviet Union, thus in effect creating 15 different bank-deposit rubles in addition to the cash ruble.[6]

Whatever its political implications (discussed below), this system at least has the merit of curbing the spillovers that made stabilization almost inconceivable under the regime that prevailed in the final months of the Soviet Union. If it helps Russia to stabilize successfully, that will satisfy one of the prime requirements for continued use of the ruble by other republics. Russia would surely also have to make an acceptable offer to share the seigniorage. Some republics might be happy to continue using the ruble under those cirumstances, perhaps even if it meant following Russia's lead on monetary policy rather than having a say in decisions on interest rates, exchange rates, reserve requirements, and credit guidelines. Indeed, given the lack of methods for financing fiscal deficits other than monetary emission, they would be constrained to follow a fiscal policy no more expansionary than that of Russia as well.

Other republics would clearly not be prepared to stick with the ruble, for the economic case is not what is driving the determination of a number of the republics—at least the Baltics, Moldova, and Ukraine—to introduce their own currencies. A separate money is viewed as an attribute of national sovereignty, and it is desired on that score rather than because of any economic arguments.

---

6. Since cash rubles are still exchangeable throughout the region, the exchange rate between cash rubles and bank-deposit rubles can be expected to vary from one state to another. So far there is no evidence that these variations are any larger than those within Russia.

Even if it is taken as given that separate monies are coming, there is a critical and disputed question regarding the timing of their introduction. In their conference papers, both Sergey Alexashenko and Inna Shteinbuka question whether it is sensible for republics to introduce their own currencies before stabilization is possible. Alexashenko goes further and argues that it would be desirable for all the states that plan to introduce their own currencies to do so simultaneously. The counterargument is that stabilization will not have a chance to get off the ground until the republics can free themselves from monetary dependence on Russia and Russia can liberate itself from the free-rider problem. If one thinks that Russia's nationalization of the ruble has already resolved the latter problem, albeit in a manner that the other republics cannot be expected to applaud, it would seem sensible for them to delay the introduction of their own currencies until they are in a position to make a serious attempt at stabilization. Whether they are in the political mood to listen to such economic advice is another matter.

Fiscal Transfers

Before turning to the political dimension alluded to above, it is convenient to examine a final economic consequence of Soviet disintegration. This is the termination of the extensive fiscal transfers that had developed, primarily to benefit the states of Central Asia.

The conference paper on the four states of Central Asia, by Rustam Narzikulov, makes it clear that the withdrawal of these transfers is seen as the central implication of Soviet disintegration in that region. In recent years consumption has exceeded net domestic material product in three of the four republics,[7] leaving the whole of government spending on goods and services, and investment, to be financed by transfers from the union. These transfers were suspended upon the breakup of the union at the end of 1991. Budget deficits without transfers would be

---

7. The exception is Turkmenistan, where consumption was some 89 percent of "produced national income" (net domestic material product) in 1989, the last year for which data are available.

around 50 percent of total government expenditures in the absence of adjustments to either revenue or expenditure.

Even if the loss of transfers is not reinforced by worsened terms of trade as a result of moving to world prices (which is not expected, as documented in the appendix), it will still be a crippling blow to the region. The Central Asian states will have no alternative but to adjust in the longer run, even if the West adds them to the list of long-term aid recipients, for Western aid programs as a percentage of the recipient's GNP (other than that from western to eastern Germany) never approach the size of the transfers that the union government was making to Central Asia. It seems that this is well understood in Central Asia, and the occasional newspaper report[8] suggests that at least some of the region's leaders see independence as an opportunity to break away from the role of hewers of wood and drawers of water assigned to them by the socialist division of labor.

Russian Dominance

The Soviet Union was essentially a perpetuation of the Russian Empire. Yet when Boris Yeltsin achieved power in Russia he dismantled that empire with none of the vacillation shown by many of the Western colonial powers (despite the encouragement he was getting from some in the West to follow Gorbachev's example in struggling to keep the union together). So far, at least, decolonization has been achieved without anything like the bloodshed that accompanied the British withdrawal from India, the French exodus from Algeria, or even the Portuguese pullout from their former domains, not to mention the savage civil war in Yugoslavia. The Russians surely deserve a measure of credit for their speedy recognition that empires belong with authoritarianism and socialism in the junkyard of history.

Russia nonetheless remains the dominant power in the region. Both the population of Russia itself and the number of Russians living

---

8. See, for example, Leyla Boulton, "Painful and Protracted Birth of a Nation," *Financial Times,* 8 May 1992.

throughout the Soviet Union amounted to just over 50 percent of the Soviet total, and the economic weight of Russia was rather larger than that. First Deputy Finance Minister Andrey Vavilov expressed the position of the present Russian government at the final session of the conference. It is a government committed to economic reform and unwilling to be held back by the hesitations of former Communists (whom the government views as being only partly reconstructed) still in office in many of the other new states. These new states themselves are showing great reluctance to pick up their share of the burdens inherited from the past, such as paying the army and cleaning up after Chernobyl. Russia too has its grievances against its partners, and it feels itself both big enough and with enough at stake to lay down the law.

It is also unsurprising that the other new states resent what they see as high-handed Russian arrogance. Time and again during the conference one heard complaints about Russian insensitivity—not just about specific actions (like the failure to supply enough ruble banknotes, or the interest charges being levied on the banknotes that are supplied), but also about the inability to negotiate with Moscow. Several states, notably Belarus and Kazakhstan, would clearly prefer to maintain close ties with Moscow, including a common currency, but feel they are being forced toward monetary independence by Russian intransigence.

This is not the sort of problem for which one can anticipate any easy or quick solution. Greater understanding is bound to take time to develop under the best of circumstances. It will have to be nurtured, by discussions and conferences in which the West can surely play an intermediating role, as well as by direct negotiations. Perhaps a good starting point would be for the Russian authorities to heed the advice of Sergey Alexashenko, who criticized the Russian authorities not so much for their actions as for their failure to give a clear lead on two key questions: the future monetary system of the region, and the future of interrepublic economic relations.

4 Alternative Payments Systems

The major policy question posed by Soviet disintegration is the nature of the payments mechanism that will be used to conduct the intratrade of the area. This is not to dismiss the crucial importance of moving to enterprise-to-enterprise trade, but rather to assert that that transition poses no controversial policy issues, except those involved in developing a satisfactory payments mechanism. Nor is it to disregard the need to provide at least transitional help to the Central Asian states in order to mitigate the costs of the big adjustments that they must undertake, but rather to suggest that that topic (which is indeed discussed subsequently) does not raise particularly novel economic issues.

The assertion of the primacy of the payments issue is intended to imply that this issue is far more crucial in limiting the collapse of intratrade than a set of trade rules would be. A commitment to free trade within the area of the former Soviet Union, or at least within the CIS, remains highly desirable.[1] The point is that any such commitment will prove to be a dead letter unless it is accompanied by an effective regime for the financing of intratrade. On the other hand, if the financial provisions for conducting and adjusting trade are operating reasonably smoothly, the pressures to restrict trade should prove containable. It may be that the best time to seek a commitment to liberal trade rules, or perhaps even to free intratrade (the "Eastern Economic Community" of Havrylyshyn and Williamson 1991), will be when the payments issue has been sorted out.

It would be quite wrong, however, to suggest that the issue of organizing payments is exclusively one that relates to interrepublic trade. On

---

1. Suggestions regarding the desirable content of a commitment to free intratrade were presented in Havrylyshyn and Williamson (1991, 24). The topic is also discussed by Nuti and Pisani-Ferry (1992), who give a brief account of a conference on the topic convened in Brussels by the Centre for European Policy Studies and the Soros Foundation in February 1992.

the contrary, the payments mechanism *within* Russia—and doubtless within the other states as well—is in a state of near-collapse. It is reported that on average the banking system takes between four and eight weeks to settle transactions. This is one reason why so much trade takes place on a barter basis, and why hard currency is also being used on a limited scale to settle transactions even within Russia.

The delays in settling payments are also one reason for the reported growth in credit extended from one enterprise to another. These delays prevent enterprises from finding out which of their customers are unwilling or unable to pay, or at least to find out quickly enough for the information to be of much use. This is bound to discourage the authorities from hardening budget constraints, for fear that the wrong enterprises might be driven into bankruptcy as a result of payments not being received promptly.

The Central Bank of Russia (and the other central banks) should surely make the restoration of a system of rapid and efficient interbank clearing one of its priorities, perhaps even its number one priority. If Western technical assistance can be of help in this regard, it should be made available as a matter of the utmost urgency. Clearly interrepublic payments are unlikely to work satisfactorily until intrarepublic payments are functioning efficiently.

Once that condition has been satisfied, there would seem to be four options for the financing of intratrade that are worth discussing: a ruble zone, a ruble area, dollar payments, and a payments union.[2] These options are explained and discussed below. The separate examination of these four options is not intended to imply that all 14 non-Russian republics are likely to select the same system: on the contrary, mixed solutions, with some states remaining at least within a ruble area and

---

2. This classification largely parallels Alexashenko's taxonomy of five options for the future organization of the monetary system in the former Soviet Union: a common ruble run by an interrepublic central bank, a Russian ruble used also by other republics (the "ruble zone"), a Russian ruble used as a currency peg (the "ruble area"), a regional arrangement like a payments union or the European Monetary System, and complete independence of national currencies. I amalgamate his first two categories and narrow the last two, since my discussion focuses exclusively on medium-run organization of payments for intratrade.

others refusing to participate even in a payments union, seem quite likely.

A Ruble Zone

By a "ruble zone" I mean an area that continues to use the ruble as a common currency. It is quite clear that not all of the former Soviet republics are willing to contemplate this solution: at least the Baltics and Ukraine plan to establish their own currencies. But some states would like to continue using the ruble, if they can reach a satisfactory agreement with Russia about the conduct of monetary policy. A major benefit of other states continuing to use the ruble is that they would be able to trade freely among themselves, and with Russia, by transferring rubles.

Or would they? At the moment all 15 republics use the ruble, yet there are limits—set by Russia's willingness to allow them to run up debts on the books of their correspondent accounts in Moscow—on the extent to which they can actually pay one another in rubles. If those limits are maintained, then sooner or later some states will presumably run out of credit and find themselves unable to continue paying their suppliers. One may think it is not much of a common money that cannot be freely used to settle debts, and that is right: since the Russian decision to require interrepublic trade to be settled through correspondent accounts, the ruble has really ceased to be a common currency. (*Cash* rubles are still common, but the bank-deposit rubles used to settle trade contracts are distinct, as argued previously.) The prevailing system is already *de facto* what is below described as a "ruble area."

To restore a ruble zone, it would be necessary for the rubles held in any one state to be usable without limit in settling debts in another state. Unless Russia's determination to stabilize its currency evaporates, that would be conceivable only if the other states renounce the right to independent policies on monetary emission. Either they must do as Russia says, which hardly seems likely, or else it will be necessary to found a federal central bank that will give the other states some say in the determination of the common monetary policy of the ruble zone. There is no sign that Russia is currently willing to contemplate such an arrangement, which means that the prospects for revival of even a limited ruble zone cannot be considered bright.

A Ruble Area

The terms "ruble zone" and "ruble area" have often been used interchangeably, but they are used here to mean two very different things. As explained above, countries within a ruble zone would continue to use the ruble as a common currency. In contrast, the term "ruble area" is meant to suggest an analogy with the sterling area in its heyday: a group of countries with separate currencies that continue to use the currency of the former "colonial" power for international purposes, even after establishing monetary independence.[3]

A major attraction of a ruble area is that in essence it already exists (or at least it will exist once the reform of the payments mechanism set in train by Russia in January 1992 is complete). The non-Russian states will all have correspondent accounts in Moscow, which they can use to receive and make payments, not just with Russia but with one another and presumably with the outside world as well. There is no reason why they should not maintain those accounts and use them in exactly the same way even if they establish their own currencies *de jure*.

The major objection to membership in a ruble zone, which was voiced in a number of the conference papers, has been that it means handing over control of monetary and fiscal policy to Moscow. This objection

---

3. The sterling area was created when Britain abandoned the gold standard in 1931; it more or less disappeared in 1968 when the remaining members demanded dollar guarantees as a condition for continuing to hold sterling in their reserves. In between the pound sterling provided the reserve currency, vehicle currency, and exchange rate peg for almost all of the Commonwealth countries (with the notable exception of Canada) and, especially prior to World War II, for a number of other countries with strong historical links with Britain. Although many of the members were colonies in the early days of the arrangement and had monetary systems based on currency boards that held sterling, they remained members of the sterling area even after achieving political independence and transforming their currency boards into central banks. In most cases they still maintained a fixed exchange rate with the pound even after achieving monetary independence, but they increasingly felt free to devalue on the basis of national considerations, and in a few cases they refused to join in when the pound was devalued.

does not apply to membership in a ruble area. The members could set their own monetary and fiscal policies, and if these turn out to give rates of inflation very different from that in Russia, the balance of payments consequences could be avoided by devaluing against the ruble (if their policies are more expansionary than those in Russia) or revaluing against it (if they succeed in mastering inflation better than does Russia). Republics could also, of course, choose to devalue not just to offset differential inflation, but also to facilitate real adjustment, which is likely to be particularly important in states that have already suffered a loss of transfer income or that will suffer a terms-of-trade loss as a result of the forthcoming energy price increases. Or, in principle at least, a republic might one day wish to revalue to facilitate real adjustment.

There seem to be two possible objections to maintaining a ruble area to finance the trade, including the intratrade, of the former Soviet republics. One is that this arrangement still gives a privileged place to Russia. So it does, at least in the sense that it gives a special place to the ruble. But it does not give Russia any special ability to dictate the stance of macroeconomic policy to the other states, which is surely what the latter have a legitimate interest in avoiding. Nor is it clear that it is likely to give Russia the "exorbitant privilege" of having its payments deficits financed by the other countries—what Charles de Gaulle used to decry when the dollar played a similar international role—for the fundamental reason that it is Russia rather than the others that is expected to run the structural surplus in the region once the price of energy has been raised. Rather, Russia is likely to suffer the burden of providing sufficient credit to make the system work. This is the sort of burden that a country with the aspiration to remain a global power can sometimes be persuaded to accept, and it would seem a rather expensive nationalistic gesture of the other states to reject a Russian offer to pick up the burden if such an offer is forthcoming.[4]

---

4. If Russia wishes to make it more attractive for the other republics to remain members of a ruble area, it might consider allowing them to use some part of the rubles they retire from circulation as they introduce their own currencies in order to build up the balances in their correspondent accounts. So far Russia has aimed to prevent Ukraine (in particular)

The other objection to a ruble area is that traditionally only stable currencies have succeeded in fulfilling the role that is here proposed for the ruble. Despite the vigor with which Yegor Gaidar and his team have pursued stabilization policies, it is still far from clear that Russia will achieve a reasonable degree of price stability in the next few months. Might a ruble area emerge despite such a failure? The answer is not clear. It is usually thought that the reason countries have always been reluctant to use an unstable currency as their vehicle and reserve currency is that they anticipated holding net balances in that currency, and since real interest rates are typically negative under high and unstable inflation, they risked suffering partial expropriation. But the situation is in this instance very different: the other states are likely to have net debit positions with Russia, which means that they will *benefit* financially from rapid Russian inflation that erodes the real value of their liabilities. Despite this factor, intuition suggests that it is unlikely that the other states would be willing to remain in a ruble area if the ruble were suffering such rapid inflation as to undermine its acceptability as money within Russia. A reasonable approximation to price stability will surely be needed.

Dollar Settlement

If there is insufficient trust among the former Soviet republics to permit continued use of the ruble to settle interrepublic trade, even in the rather undemanding form of a ruble area, then the natural inclination

---

from spending the rubles withdrawn from circulation on Russian goods—a threat that at one stage looked quite real but that Ukrainian representatives forswore at a meeting in Brussels in February 1992 (the text of the agreement reached is printed in IMF 1992, appendix III). The Russian demand that other republics keep rubles that are no longer needed elsewhere from being spent in Russia is understandable, although there is also a counterargument that this might compensate the other republics for the loss of seigniorage they have suffered since Russia nationalized the ruble. Quite apart from equity issues, however, it might make sense for Russia to agree to credit (say) 10 percent of the value of the returned ruble banknotes to the correspondent accounts, both as an inducement to stay in the ruble area and as an incentive to do a thorough job of converting all cash rubles held in other republics into the new local currencies.

after the establishment of separate currencies will be to settle trade by the use of dollars (or another hard currency). Indeed, this is apparently already happening to some extent, especially with trade contracted through the commercial exchanges. It is also what happened to trade among the former CMEA members after that organization was abolished.

The problem with dollar settlement is that it requires substantial reserves of hard currency. The sums involved are not as large as they would be if the dollar were adopted as the local currency ("dollarization"), something that tends to happen spontaneously when inflation gets out of hand, and has indeed been happening at the margin in the former Soviet Union already. Nor are they as large as is required by a currency board arrangement, which essentially requires as many dollars as dollarization does, although it is much less expensive in flow terms because the dollars are held as interest-earning assets by the currency board rather than a large part of them being held in the form of non-interest-earning dollar bills by the general public.

How many dollars would be required if the economies of the former Soviet republics were completely dollarized (or, alternatively, if all the republics established currency boards)? On the basis of an exchange rate consistent with the fundamentals, Soviet GNP was at least $500 billion before the collapse started. The joint study by the IMF, the World Bank, the Organization for Economic Cooperation and Development (OECD), and the European Bank for Reconstruction and Development (1991, table K.8, 132) states that currency in circulation amounted to 133 billion rubles at the end of 1990, a year in which GNP was a trillion rubles; other monetary assets totaled 614 billion rubles. If those other assets required a 10 percent reserve in the form of external dollars, the total dollar requirement would be more than $100 billion[5]—a lot of money for a bankrupt group of states that cannot even service their external debt.[6]

---

5. That is, 13 percent of $500 billion, plus 10 percent of 61 percent of $500 billion.

6. Some advocates of currency boards (Hanke and Schuler 1991) have come up with dramatically lower numbers, but they do so by translating ex-Soviet monetary needs into dollars at the prevailing exchange rate, which grossly undervalues the ruble. If a currency

Although dollar settlement of trade would not be nearly as expensive as dollarization or a currency board, it would still need a lot of dollars. Interrepublic trade was 21 percent of Soviet GDP in 1988 (IMF et al. 1991, table 26, 225), or about $100 billion. A common rule of thumb in the days of the Bretton Woods system was that countries needed to keep a reserves-imports ratio of at least 30 percent, suggesting that a minimum of $30 billion would be needed to finance intratrade (plus a reserve for external trade). (If reserves are not centralized in the central bank as they were in the days of Bretton Woods, then the need would be larger, because economies of scale in reserve-holding would not be realized.)

Even though the Soviet Union went bankrupt at the end of 1991 and its successor states have not built up much in the way of reserves since, there may actually be a nonnegligible stock of dollars available to finance trade. It was the Institute of International Finance (1992) that first drew attention to the evidence of massive capital flight from the Soviet Union. Most observers felt that their estimate of some $14 billion being held abroad was exaggerated, but the IMF estimate that the Soviet Union had an overall surplus of almost $5 billion in convertible currencies in 1991 (in a year when it suffered a heavy loss of reserves) confirms that capital flight must have been substantial. Since that flight overwhelmingly takes the form of enterprises building up hard-currency holdings in Western bank accounts rather than remitting all their earnings, the money is in a form that would be readily available to finance trade.

Even allowing for the ability to mobilize flight capital, however, the former Soviet republics would fall far short of the amount of hard currency needed to assure them of reserve ease. Hence the consequence of resorting to dollar settlement would probably be restrictions of "inessential" imports designed to save scarce foreign exchange, even if the victims of the restrictions are other republics that are just as short of hard currency. That is exactly the sort of paralysis of trade from which

---

board fulfilled their expectations and restored confidence in the ruble, the need would rise to the sort of level calculated above. The economy would go into recession until it could import enough dollars to satisfy the demand for money.

Western Europe suffered in the early postwar years, before Marshall Plan conditionality and the European Payments Union (EPU) induced intra-European liberalization.

A Clearing or Payments Union

The EPU precedent naturally raises the question as to whether a similar arrangement might not be worthwhile in the former Soviet Union today. Could it combine the advantages of denominating trade and debts in a hard currency, and the discipline of knowing that ultimate settlement would be in hard currency, with a saving in foreign exchange that would avoid the danger of republics restricting their imports from one another?[7]

A clearing union is an arrangement in which the member countries agree to accept one another's currencies in payment for exports, deposit their earnings from those exports with the agent of the union, allow the claims to be consolidated and periodically netted out on a multilateral basis, and then settle the remaining imbalances centrally with the union in hard currency. This arrangement permits the establishment or maintenance of current account convertibility while achieving major economies in the need for hard-currency reserves because it is only net imbalances that have to be settled in hard currency, rather than each individual transaction. A payments union has the additional feature that the resulting imbalances are settled in a mixture of credit and hard currencies, thus further economizing on the need for hard-currency reserves.

It is often said that a clearing or payments union would be redundant if the republics all established current account convertibility. This view is mistaken. In order to establish convertibility in the former Soviet republics without a payments union, it would be necessary to have reserves approaching five times as high as would be needed with such

---

7. Jozef M. van Brabant (1991) has been the most forceful advocate of a Central European Payments Union; he argued the case for a similar arrangement among the former Soviet republics during the Vienna conference.

a union, given that about 80 percent of trade is intratrade. In fact, a payments union is still a sensible arrangement among countries that have established current account convertibility with the rest of the world, if they trade intensively among themselves and have a shortage of hard currency. It can enable them not only to establish current account convertibility among themselves, but also to establish it with the rest of the world more rapidly than would otherwise be feasible, and/or avoid as sharp a depreciation of their currencies as would otherwise be necessary. Once reserves are no longer in short supply, a payments union becomes redundant; it can be phased out gradually, as the EPU was, by periodically increasing the proportion of hard currency used in settlement.

There is no technical difficulty in combining payment through a payments union for one group of countries with payment in dollars to another, as long as exchange controls still exist so that an importer has to demonstrate a foreign purchase before he or she is entitled to buy dollars. If the purchase is from a supplier within the region covered by the payments union, the purchaser is channeled through that mechanism rather than allowed access to dollars. The feasibility of this arrangement is demonstrated by the fact that it was operated by Switzerland, which had current account convertibility with the dollar area, at the time when it was also a member of the EPU.

Nor does a payments union require fixed exchange rates among the participants. That was the basis on which the EPU functioned, but it would be quite possible to operate a clearing union among countries with floating currencies or frequently adjusted pegs. Under those conditions the exact date when a transaction was entered on the books of the clearing agent would acquire a significance that was absent in the case of the EPU, but that would not constitute a decisive obstacle to the functioning of the system.

Should the members of a payments union be expected to aim at overall payments balance only, or should they also seek to balance their intraunion payments? In the case of the EPU this issue was attenuated by the fact that a very large share of the members' trade originated within the EPU area (which included the colonial empires of the European powers). Despite this, members did aim at intraunion as well as overall balance. They had a separate policy variable that they could deploy to aim at the additional objective, inasmuch as quantitative restrictions on trade were still prevalent and more severe against the dollar area than within the EPU area. A payments union covering the successor states of the Soviet Union would probably need to operate on the alternative principle, at least if Russia and other republics fulfill their declared intention of moving quickly to current account convertibility with the outside world. That is, in the absence of a policy that could be used differentially by individual republics, or in common by all of them together, members will have to aim at overall balance. This implies that a member that has a surplus with the outside world would have to use its net dollar earnings to finance its intra-area deficit. Conversely, a member with an external deficit offset by a surplus within the area would have to be allowed to use its creditor position within the union to finance its external deficit.

Another question that is sometimes raised is the scope of membership, notably whether former CMEA members in Central and Eastern Europe, and Mongolia, should be invited to participate. Their inclusion would seem to offer a chance of reversing the drastic decline in trade that followed the move to hard-currency financing at the start of 1991. Now that the geopolitical fear of continued Soviet domination that underlay their refusal to contemplate such arrangements when they were first proposed in 1990 has vanished, and the countries of Central and Eastern Europe have experienced the hardship caused by the disappearance of Soviet orders, one might have expected the idea to be welcomed in the non-Soviet former CMEA members. In fact, for reasons that are not fully clear, there seems no weakening in their hostility to the idea. They surely do not believe that the new Russia is a threat comparable to the old Soviet Union. Perhaps they have not grasped the point made above about the feasibility of combining membership in a payments union with one group of countries and current account convertibility with another.

5 Policy Recommendations

It was argued above that, even though the total trade of the ex-Soviet republics will and should diminish in the long run, and even though the share of intratrade in that diminished total will and should likewise decline, an excessive and precipitate fall could give a further vicious twist to the downward spiral in which the region is currently trapped. This is not only a theoretical possibility, but something that the fragmentary evidence available indicates is actually happening. Historical precedents (not to mention common sense) suggest that it would be worth trying to arrest and reverse this development, and that outside influence might be of strategic importance in doing so.

Hence it is appropriate to turn to a discussion of what it would be sensible for the governments of the former Soviet republics to do, and of the extent to which the West should push them to act on that advice. The discussion starts by considering the central issue of the payments system, and goes on to consider two other topics—transfers and aid, and currency stabilization—the resolution of which is also critical to relations among the republics.

The Payments System

Of the four options for settling interrepublic transactions discussed in the previous section, a ruble zone will certainly not be acceptable to all the new states, because some of them have made a firm political commitment to introduce their own monies. The rump of a ruble zone may survive if the Russians succeed in stabilizing, and especially if they can bring themselves to share the seigniorage and to give the other participants a genuine share in monetary decision making, but it will not solve the main problem because its membership will be too restricted.

It seems that the IMF is having some difficulty in acknowledging this reality. Its latest publication on the subject, the April 1992 volume on

Common Issues and Interrepublic Relations in the Former USSR in the *Economic Review* series resulting from the premembership negotiations, continues to hanker after a ruble zone. It even asserts (IMF 1992, 20) that one of the disadvantages of a payments union is that "there is an element of moral hazard involved: a payments union would reduce the potential costs—in terms of trade disruption—of moving to a separate currency and might therefore encourage some of the ruble-based republics to move more quickly towards national. . .currencies." Unless the Russian attitude to sharing seigniorage and monetary sovereignty changes markedly, the IMF is pushing a hopeless cause. Moreover, it is not even clear that we should welcome a Russian willingness to share monetary (and fiscal) sovereignty at this point, since it could all too easily involve a dilution from the Russian government's commitment to stabilization.

The other option that should be resisted is full settlement in dollars or any other hard currency. Even though ex-Soviet enterprises now have quite a few dollars in Western banks as a result of capital flight, there would not be enough to avoid strong contractionary pressures on intratrade. Moreover, it is more sensible to plan a system that, once it reestablishes confidence, will enable those dollars to be mobilized for productive purposes than to design one that will require yet more dollars to be earned as a condition for reviving output.

That leaves two options: a ruble area and a payments union. Either of these could support multilateral trade among enterprises without calling for vast sums of hard currency that the republics do not have and without requiring them to forgo or share monetary sovereignty. The West does not have a strong interest in seeing one of those solutions adopted rather than the other, but it surely does have a crucial interest in seeing one *or* the other implemented. It should therefore be prepared to give such financial support as may be needed to get one or the other off the ground, and it might reasonably hesitate to put in a lot of money unless the ex-Soviets can get their act together to the point of agreeing on one of these two mechanisms.

The ex-Soviet republics might, however, find difficulty in reaching agreement on this issue. If Russia favored a ruble area, it might refuse to join a payments union—which would make no sense without Russian participation—in an attempt to force the other republics to go along. But this is a topic where the primary responsibility for deciding which system to adopt should surely be that of the non-Russian republics. It would be well and good if Russia can persuade them that it is in their interests to remain within a ruble area (and Russia does have some weapons that it can deploy for that purpose, such as the amount of credit it would be prepared to advance and the extent to which it might credit the correspondent accounts of the republics for ruble banknotes withdrawn from circulation). If Russia fails to persuade them, then the West should use moral suasion to induce Russia to participate in a payments union.

The form of the financial support would be very different depending on which solution was adopted. To make a ruble area work, the key need—despite the argument that indebted republics might not mind too much if their ruble liabilities were eroded by inflation—is to stabilize the ruble. The possible role of a stabilization fund in achieving that objective is discussed below. With a payments union solution, in contrast, ruble stabilization would be a matter of national interest to Russia rather than of systemic interest to all the new states. The key systemic need would instead be for a capital fund that would permit the payments union to extend more credit to those states in cumulative deficit than it would need to obtain from those in cumulative surplus.

It turns out that such a fund set up on the same relative scale as that which catalyzed the EPU would require the surprisingly modest sum of $1.3 billion if it were restricted to the former Soviet republics, or $2.5 billion in the unlikely event that it was extended to include the other former members of the CMEA (Havrylyshyn and Williamson 1991, 58). But a case can be made for a substantially larger fund than that. In the first place, it can be argued that the EPU was somewhat underfunded, for there were instances of countries that exhausted their credits even though the imbalances involved were expected to be—and proved to be—temporary and reversible. Germany in 1950–51 was the outstanding case in point (Kaplan and Schleiminger 1989, chapter 6). Second, a key objective of reform is to institute the replacement of interstate barter agreements by enterprise-to-enterprise trade, and very tight balance of payments constraints seem unlikely to be consistent with a rapid move in that direction.

The purpose of a payments union is to provide swing credits to finance the bulk of the short-term variations in net balances inherent in reasonably free trade. (The credits finance less than 100 percent of those imbalances to make sure that participants have an incentive to take adjustment action promptly once imbalances that are not expected to reverse themselves become apparent. That incentive will probably need to be reinforced by a vigilant IMF if republics are to resist the temptation to let things ride until a crisis develops, in the hope that a deficit will reverse itself naturally.) A payments union cannot finance structural imbalances, and any attempt to rely on it for that purpose would simply guarantee an early crisis as the structural deficit countries exhausted their credit limits. This does not mean that structural deficit countries cannot participate in a payments union, but simply that the size of the structural deficit that they will be allowed to run must be determined *ex ante* and then financed from outside sources. Each year they would then receive a credit in the accounts of the payments union equal to the finance provided from outside, and a deficit on the books of the payments union would arise only if their total deficit exceeded the size of that credit.

Transfers and Aid

Obviously two crucial questions are to whom such credits might be made available and from where the finance might come. Note that this issue is not specific to a payments union, but would arise also with a ruble area. If structural deficit states fail to get finance, then in that system too they will be faced with a need to adjust when they reach the credit limit that Russia is willing to permit. A difference would arise only insofar as Russia might be willing to be less (or more) generous in allowing credit within a ruble area than in financing structural deficits in association with a payments union. The usual argument has been that the leavening of outside credit in a payments union can help to persuade the structural surplus countries to extend more credit through a payments union than they would otherwise be willing to sanction, but it could be that the reverse would be true in the present instance, inasmuch as a ruble area might appeal to Russian pride.

   Two groups of countries seem all too likely to emerge as structural deficit countries for the next few years. The first consists of the Central Asian republics, which had become large recipients of transfers from the union government. As already argued, there is no way that these states are going to continue receiving aid on the scale of recent transfers in the long run. Presumably the West will add them to the list of developing countries eligible to receive aid, but that will replace no more than a fraction of what they had been getting from the union government. Instead of the 25 percent of GDP, or more, that they were receiving, they can expect perhaps 5 percent on a continuing basis.[1] The balance will have to be adjusted. But there is a limit to the speed with which adjustment can be effected if it is to take the efficient form of developing new tradeable-goods industries rather than the wasteful form of repressing demand, and adjustment of that efficient form is feasible only if there is finance for the deficit that will persist in the interim while the structure of productive capacity is being changed.

Even if this basic argument for providing finance for temporary structural deficits on the part of the Central Asian states is accepted, two issues remain. One is the size and duration of the aid. Presumably it should start out at some substantial fraction (half? two-thirds? three-quarters?) of the level of the former transfers whose withdrawal has caused the problem, and should then progressively decrease over a normal planning horizon (perhaps five years). The figures in table A.1 in the appendix imply that the combined net material product (NMP) of the four Central Asian states was about 5.5 percent of that of the Soviet Union as a whole. If the proportion of GDP was similar, it would have been around $30 billion, which would mean that transfers were formerly running at something like $7 billion per year. Replacing 60 percent of those transfers in the first year would thus cost about $4 billion, a sum that would then decrease progressively in future years.

As to the sources of the aid, it can be argued that Russia should be a major contributor, since Russia will get a windfall benefit from energy price increases. On the other hand, Russia itself is a candidate for substantial aid in the short term. Might it not make sense for the West to give a part of that aid not directly to Russia, but in the form of grants

---

1. Five percent of the recipient's GDP is a typical level of aid both for low-income countries and for the poorer members of the European Community to receive from Brussels.

to the Central Asians that they can use to finance structural deficits with Russia? This would allow Russia to earn some of its dollars through trade, reducing the risk that it might become aid-dependent.

The second group of countries that may emerge as structural deficit countries in the next few years consists of those that will be adversely impacted by the energy price increases. According to the (Soviet) estimates cited in the joint study (IMF et al. 1991, table 27, 226), these are Belarus (with an adverse impact of 16 percent of NMP expected from the switch to world prices), Moldova (20 percent), the Baltics (adverse impacts of 15 percent to 24 percent), and the Caucasians (with costs estimated as varying between a surprisingly modest 5 percent of NMP in Armenia to 15 percent in Azerbaijan).

The case for providing interim finance to these states is similar to, although not as compelling as, that developed above for helping the Central Asians to soften the brutality of the adjustment process. It is less compelling for two reasons: because the economies are more diversified and should therefore be better placed to adjust reasonably quickly, and because living standards are not as low (except in Azerbaijan). In view of these differences, it might make sense to help these countries by increasing the credit provided through a payments union (or by a deal whereby Russia would enlarge their credit limits in a ruble area in return for additional aid), rather than assuming that they are predestined to be structural deficit countries.

That leaves three of the new states that are not affected by adverse shocks emanating from the dissolution of the Soviet Union. They happen to be the three largest republics in economic terms: Russia, Ukraine, and Kazakhstan. Of course, all three are heavily affected by the shocks that have resulted from the collapse of the Communist system. The West has already accepted the case for helping them make the transition to a market economy by giving substantial financial help: for example, Michel Camdessus, the Managing Director of the IMF, has spoken of a financing requirement for Russia alone of $20 billion to $25 billion in 1992, plus another $20 billion or so for the other republics (Camdessus 1992).

The Russian aid includes a sum of $6 billion for a stabilization fund, which would serve systemic rather than just Russian interests if intratrade were financed in rubles. This Western willingness to support a

Russian stabilization fund is consistent with the IMF's enthusiasm for maintenance of a ruble zone. But the strategy of concentrating on stabilizing the ruble first would also be appropriate if a decision were made to finance intratrade through a ruble area.

If Russia does not come acceptably close to stabilizing inflation, then neither a ruble zone nor a ruble area is likely to survive for long. C. Fred Bergsten suggested in Vienna that in that event the G-7 might divert the resources that have been set aside for a stabilization fund in order to endow a payments union instead. Obviously that would be feasible only if Russia has not already received the stabilization fund and used it in an unsuccessful attempt to stabilize the ruble. This provides yet another reason for not triggering the release of the stabilization fund until Russia has a program that deserves support. But some risks will have to be taken, and if worst comes to worst that the West may have to put together a second fund. Or the other republics may choose a payments union even if Russia does succeed in stabilizing, which would also require a second fund.

More generally, it seems important to recognize that an aid program for the former Soviet republics ought to be fashioned to acknowledge the fundamental differences in their situations. The collapse in Russia has been particularly severe, and it therefore makes sense to contemplate substantial aid. But Russia has enormous natural resources that are easily saleable on world markets, and so a relatively rapid return to financial self-sufficiency ought to be feasible. Indeed, it can expect to be benefiting from improved terms of trade as a result of higher prices for its energy exports to the other republics already by 1993.

What Russia needs really is something like a Marshall Plan: a substantial but relatively brief injection of external funds, on the condition that it get together with its neighbors to create an environment that will permit efficient intratrade to flourish. One way of doing that is to give the Central Asian states the funds they will need in the short run to allow an efficient adjustment program, and then allow Russia to earn hard currency from them by selling its oil. Drawing the analogy with the Marshall Plan should do something to limit the assault on Russian pride implied by accepting aid. The analogy also suggests that the intention to provide almost all of the help in the form of loans at market interest rates ought to be reviewed; Western Europe was given grants and thus avoided a debt buildup such as now threatens the former Soviet republics.

Central Asia is at the other extreme. It is likely to need a continuing aid program for many years, but the amounts involved are not excessive. A "typical" aid level of around 5 percent of the recipients' GDP would cost under $2 billion per year. Even an additional adjustment program that started off at $4 billion per year would not be unmanageably large, especially if Japan agrees to accept prime responsibility for helping this region.

The other republics are likely to require intermediate treatment. They do not have the natural resources that will permit a rapid balance of payments turnround,[2] but neither are they so backward as to justify a long-term continuing aid program. A reasonable objective might be to restore self-reliance within a decade.

A part of any aid program will take the form of debt restructuring. The G-7's record on this topic has so far been abysmal: it spent the autumn of 1991, when all the former Soviet republics should have been concentrating on the strategic design of their programs for moving to a market economy, in bullying the new republics to sign on to the formula—for which there is no historical precedent—that they will be "jointly and severally" responsible for the debt of the former Soviet Union. The G-7 did ultimately, if grudgingly, concede the reality that repayment of a year's debt principal would have to be deferred, but it insisted on continued payment of interest, arguing that suspending such payments would make the republics ineligible to receive new credits. Since it is only their own rules that prevent new credits being granted to a country in arrears on interest payments, this is lame.

The situation demands a much bolder initiative, although not in the form of generalized debt relief. On the contrary, the level of debt—

---

2. However, several of the Russian authors at the conference seemed to believe that the minimal level of current exports to the rest of the world, and the absence of natural resources that would permit a quick expansion in such exports, would necessarily preclude their ability to establish independent currencies. This is the wrong criterion: what matters is their *overall* balance rather than their bilateral balance with the countries outside of the former Soviet Union.

something like $68 billion—remains modest in comparison with the size of the region's economy, so a Brady-style debt reduction is not called for. Some republics may ultimately need that, but it is not possible to forecast which may find themselves in that situation at the current time. What is transparently clear is that there is a chronic liquidity problem, which is not going to disappear quickly, and attempts to extract debt service in the next few years are just going to divert effort from more urgent subjects.

The right solution is to abandon the "jointly and severally" formula, restructure the debt of each republic to give (say) 10 years grace and 10 years of interest capitalization, and then come back in a decade's time to see which republics are in a position to accept their obligations and which will have to be granted debt reduction. Given the fundamental strengths in Russia's position, one would expect Russia to be among those able to accept their obligations.

Stabilization

The fact that a successful ruble area is unlikely to develop without a successful stabilization of the ruble makes it appropriate to add a few words on that topic.

Russia has already taken strong action in 1992 to bring the budget deficit under control. It is unlikely that the deficit will come down as far as was originally targeted (1 percent of GDP), but the fiscal accounts should be in an acceptable state provided the government succeeds in appropriating a reasonable part of the rents from increased energy prices.

The other central elements of a stabilization program remain to be addressed. In the first place, monetary control has still not been achieved. It has been impeded by several factors. One was the ambiguous commitment of the former governor of the central bank, who reported to parliament rather than to the economic team in the government and who made use of his independence to reduce the threat that hard budget constraints would drive enterprises to bankruptcy. As this goes to press it remains to be seen who will be appointed in his place following his resignation in early June 1992, and whether the successor will enforce monetary policy more stringently. Another factor is the lack of an efficient interbank settlements system, which leads to unreasonable delays in payments and thus impedes the enforcement of hard budget constraints because of the large random element in how they would bite, as well as contributing to the explosion in interenterprise credit. That is reinforced by the incentive to exploit such credit that arises from the fact that it is interest-free. The least that needs to be done is to modernize the interbank settlement system and to index the nominal value of these interenterprise credits to the price level (so that the real interest rate would rise at least to zero).

Apart from the lack of an incomes policy, a subject on which the author has no helpful suggestions to offer, the other big problem is the lack of a stable exchange rate at a level supportive of price stability. At present there are still several exchange rates, all of them—including the most important, the one that most enterprises use to pay for their imports—sharply undervaluing the ruble. At the beginning of 1992, the main ruble rate was around 100 to the dollar, at a time when the average wage was just under 1,000 rubles per month. Russian labor may be worth as little as $100 per month until the economy begins to get back on its feet, but it is certainly worth more than $10 per month! In other words, the exchange rate was perhaps ten times a rate that would have made sense in terms of the fundamentals.

The IMF describes this rate as a "quasi-floating market rate," presumably on the ground that the rate chosen in the winter of 1991–92 (and maintained until the spring, when it underwent a modest appreciation) was more or less the same as the rate prevailing on the parallel market when it was chosen. But one thing that we have surely learned by now from the experience of other economies in transition from socialism—notably Poland and Czechoslovakia—is that to make official a rate established on the black market prior to stabilization and liberalization is almost to guarantee that the currency will be valued far too low to be compatible with macroeconomic stability. Because the currency is so undervalued, there are strong arbitrage pressures pushing prices upward.

It would be wrong to dismiss these pressures just because the Soviet economy was relatively closed. Peter Dittus of the OECD mentioned at the Vienna conference that statistics gathered by his organization suggested that Soviet non-raw-materials exports had almost doubled in

1991; this implies that at least some enterprises are already capable of responding to price incentives coming from the exchange rate. The experience of rising prices stimulates wage demands, nurtures inflationary expectations, and encourages the development of other sources of inflationary momentum such as indexation. At the same time, however, the price increases reduce real demand: through squeezing real wages, through creating paper profits on inventory appreciation that are then taxed at a high rate, through reducing the real value of the money supply (the real balance effect), and doubtless through hurting confidence as well. Thus the macroeconomic effect of an acutely undervalued currency is highly stagflationary.

Let it be repeated once more that this is not a hypothetical danger, but rather what some of us regard as the major mistake so far identified in the design of the transition (see, for example, Portes 1992, Williamson 1992a). Yet it looks as though Russia may be going to repeat the blunder. The Russian government currently indicates that the various exchange rates will be unified on 1 July 1992, and access of the typical Russian enterprise to foreign exchange will be eased (which requires making dollars available *quickly*), to the point where current account convertibility can be said to be established.

That is a bold and sensible proposal, but it will not support macroeconomic stability unless the unified exchange rate is at a level consistent with the fundamentals. Here the announced intentions are less reassuring. Initially the exchange rate is to be allowed to float, with the intention of finding where it should be fixed (but with the hope expressed by at least some officials that the rate will float to a rate of around 80 rubles to the dollar). If floating exchange rates could be relied on to float to levels that would support macroeconomic stabilization, there would be little point in thinking of fixing them at all. But unfortunately no such presumption exists. On the contrary, if the authorities have enough credibility to be able to contemplate fixing the rate, then the presumption is that the rate will float to where the market thinks the authorities are going to fix it!

Hence the relevant question is whether 80 rubles to the dollar will be a sensible rate to fix come September 1992. As usual it is fairly difficult to say anything very conclusive about what the right rate will be, but it is possible to narrow the range of uncertainty by saying something

about what rates would be wrong. And surely any rate that tries to establish a Russian real wage of substantially under $100 per month can be described as unambiguously wrong. Since the average Russian wage was just under 1,000 rubles per month in January 1992, an exchange rate of 80 rubles to the dollar will on that criterion leave the ruble undervalued unless nominal wages multiply by eight times in nine months. Despite all Russia's current problems, that seems unlikely.

If the announced intentions are a recipe for worsening stagflation, what would be preferable? One cannot simply announce that the rate will be stabilized at 30 or 40 rubles to the dollar and rely on it to go there, because the market will not regard as credible so large an appreciation from the rates that have prevailed for months. The Russian authorities are in fact justified in planning to require the rate to float to where it is going to be fixed, to make sure that it is a rate that can command credibility. But suppose that the rate at which they want to fix it is one that the market will not find credible. What then?

The most hopeful approach would seem to be to announce where the authorities want the rate to go, and then stand ready to intervene to encourage it to move in that direction, without either accepting an obligation to intervene (which could prove prohibitively expensive until credibility has built up) or pretending that the market knows best and all they are doing is planning to endorse its judgment. If holders of flight capital once begin to see that the ruble is appreciating and understand that it may have a lot further to go, they will want to move back in before the bulk of the appreciation actually happens (at least so long as they know that current account convertibility really has been established, so that they will be able to buy back foreign exchange when they need it in order to buy imports). What looks credible may change very quickly. But note that this strategy would demand a modification in the announced intention of the G-7, which is to release the stabilization fund only *after* the ruble has been stabilized. Russia will need the stabilization fund before stabilization is achieved in order to be able to intervene to start the appreciation. It remains essential that the stabilization fund not be disbursed until all the conditions needed to permit stabilization other than a realistic exchange rate—including an efficient system of interbank settlement—are in place.

Such a strategy is unlikely to succeed unless Russia is a lot bolder than it has been yet in dismantling the restrictions on foreign-exchange inflows. At present Russia has almost no restrictions on *imports,* but it discourages *exports* with surrender requirements, export taxes, export licenses, export quotas, and sundry red tape.[3] The motivation is obvious enough: it seems intolerable that Russia's relatively few exporters should get the windfall profits available from selling on the world market at a hyperdepreciated exchange rate goods that are scarce at home. There is similar resistance to allowing foreign direct investment to come in at the present exchange rate, which indeed implies a fire sale of Russian assets.

But fending off these inflows by creating bureaucratic obstacles to foreign investment is a thoroughly mistaken response. The right policy would be to sweep away almost all the obstacles to exports[4] and to foreign investment and allow the pioneers to reap windfall profits. Others will soon decide that they want to get in on the act before it is too late, and the resulting inflow into the ruble will take the exchange rate back to a value that reduces profitability to more normal levels. Indeed, the challenge to the Russian authorities might soon become to recognize that it is time to stop the real appreciation of the ruble before it eliminates the incentives that will place Russia firmly on the path of export-led growth. But Russia will never have to face that relatively pleasant dilemma if it continues to fret about anyone making a profit out of the foreign sector. It should follow the example set by Kazakhstan when the latter approved the deal with Chevron despite its misgiving about whether the terms were fair.

It is of critical importance that any stabilized exchange rate for the ruble be, and remain, a highly competitive rate, so as to stimulate the growth of Russian exports and investment in new export industries. This indicates the desirability of the Russian government making an early commitment to a crawling peg that would prevent future inflation from leading to overvaluation.

---

3. See Goldberg (1992) for a description of some of the impediments to Russian exporters.

4. A temporary export tax on energy has long been accepted by most Western economists as a sensible way of easing the transition: see, for example, the policy recommendations of the joint study of the IMF et al. (1990).

6 Concluding Comments

It remains to summarize the answers that have been implied in the course of this study to the set of questions laid out at the beginning.

The first of those questions was, Will market-determined trade between independent states continue with the same intensity, and in the same direction, as that inherited from the Soviet Union? The answer suggested was that in the long run the total volume of trade is likely to decline, and that there will be a dramatic shift in the composition of trade, with much less intratrade among the former Soviet republics than before and much more trade between each of them and the West.

The second question was, Is there a danger of intratrade collapsing, and how severe would the consequences be? The evidence that a collapse is in process is still somewhat fragmentary, but it is nonetheless sufficiently widespread to demand a prompt response. Similarly, the evidence that this collapse will further intensify the downward spiral in economic activity is a little on the casual side, but so many fears were expressed on this score that it would be the height of irresponsibility to dismiss the concern until the consequences can be more conclusively documented. In particular, it is wrong to argue that, because of the expectation of a long-run decline in intratrade in the course of a move to the market economy, the sooner the decline comes the better. However inefficient current practices may be, it is better that any activity that produces positive value added continue until it is possible to make the investments that will permit the factors it employs to be redeployed into new activities.

The third question was, What policy measures might avert the danger of a collapse in trade, while helping to shift it to a market basis? It was argued that the current interstate barter agreements need to be phased out quickly, and that support needs to be given to allowing enterprises to trade directly with one another. The primary issue on which that focuses attention is the system for effecting payments between republics. The first priority in this area should be to improve the intrarepublic interbank system of settlement, which is currently subject to extreme delay.

The next priority is to choose a mechanism for effecting interrepublic payments. It was urged that the IMF and the G-7 abandon their hankering after a ruble zone, which has already *de facto* broken down as a result of Russia's decision to channel interrepublic payments through a set of correspondent accounts in Moscow. It was also argued that any resort to hard currency to settle trade would be likely to induce strong pressures to restrict trade as republics attempted to compensate for their reserve shortages.

The two more promising ways to finance trade would involve either a ruble area, modeled on the sterling area of the British Commonwealth (and thus permitting each of the republics whatever degree of monetary independence it chooses), or a payments union. The West has a strong interest in ensuring that one of those arrangements is implemented, but the choice between the two is primarily one for the non-Russian republics to make. It would be quite legitimate for Russia to offer them inducements (like generous credit limits or credits for ruble banknotes when these are withdrawn from circulation and returned to the Central Bank of Russia) to stay in a ruble area, but the West should dissuade Russia from trying to railroad them into a ruble area by refusing to join a payments union.

If a ruble area is chosen, then a successful early Russian stabilization of the currency acquires importance for the whole of the Soviet Union rather than only Russia. This justifies the stabilization fund that has been proposed for Russia once Russia has a program that deserves to be backed—but such funding should be made available *before* the ruble exchange rate is fixed, so that the fund can be used to induce an appreciation of the ruble to a level that does not carry the same threat of stagflation as would a rate in the vicinity of that currently prevailing. Achieving such an appreciation will also require that Russia scrap most of its current deterrents to exporting and to inward direct investment.

If a payments union is chosen instead, the Western democracies should be prepared to endow it with a capital fund of several billion dollars. Such an endowment, which would be proportionately larger than that which the United States gave to start the European Payments

Union, would be justified as a way for the West to help those republics that are heavy net importers of energy while they adjust to the increased price of their energy imports. If the reason for selecting a payments union were that Russia had failed to stabilize and if the stabilization fund were still intact, it could be diverted to this function.

Neither a ruble area nor a payments union will suffice to render bearable the adjustment problem facing the states of Central Asia as a result of the withdrawal of their past fiscal transfers. This is another burden that the West should pick up, although with a level of aid that is phased down over five years or so. Since Russia would earn most of that hard currency through its energy exports to the region, aid to these republics would reduce the need for direct aid to Russia.

The final question posed in the introduction was, How much interest do the new states have in maintaining cooperative relationships among themselves, and what institutional forms might that cooperation take? Most participants at the Vienna conference seemed to feel that continued cooperation was important, especially in the short run until production and trade can adapt to the requirements of a market economy and integration into the wider world, but there is clearly a danger of tensions over Russia's role jeopardizing that cooperation. In the short run the most important form of cooperation is to institute an interrepublic payments mechanism that allows multilateral and enterprise-to-enterprise trade to flourish without requiring excessive quantities of hard currency.

Once that mechanism is functioning satisfactorily, it will be time to think about the institutional form of longer-term cooperative arrangements. Russia and its neighbors have to learn to interact in a forum that provides a judicious combination of nominal equality with a realistic acceptance of actual differences in power, that embodies an agreed set of principles defining the ends being sought, and that generates strong pressures to reach agreement. This forum will have to combine the roles filled in the West after World War II by the IMF and the Organization for European Economic Cooperation: those institutions provided a civilized and principled way for the United States to exert its power while paying decent attention to the interests and concerns of its smaller partners, but it also pressured the Western Europeans to act together in their common interest. One of the first tasks of such an institution established for the former Soviet Union should be to create an economic community that will allow intratrade to develop on a liberal basis. If the CIS cannot be adapted to play this role, it should be disbanded and replaced.

The euphoria that followed the defeat of the attempted coup of August 1991 has long since dissipated. No one now imagines that the massive social transformations being sought in what used to be the Soviet Union will be easy, quick, or painless. But nothing that has happened in the past year suggests them to be either impossible or undesirable. They remain perhaps the greatest challenge to our age.

Appendix: The New States

This appendix provides a sketch of the salient economic characteristics and recent policies of each of the 15 republics of the former Soviet Union. It starts with the two most important players, Russia and Ukraine, and then moves through the other Slavic states, the Baltic states, the Caucasus, Kazakhstan, and finally Central Asia.

Russia

By far the largest of the former Soviet republics is Russia. It comprises about 76 percent of the territory of the former Soviet Union (table A.1), which makes it still easily the largest country in area in the world. Russia also had about 51 percent of the Soviet population in 1990, produced about 60 percent of Soviet GDP and over 80 percent of its energy, and was responsible for over 75 percent of the Soviet Union's exports to the rest of the world. Per capita income was somewhat above the average for the union, although the conference paper by Nikolai Petrakov claimed that Russia has less than the average per capita *consumption*, especially of foodstuffs. Russia had a disproportionate share of the military industries, especially around Leningrad (now once again St. Petersburg) and in its industrial heartland around the Urals.

Table A.1 shows official estimates of population, net material product (NMP), and per capita income as a percentage of the Soviet average, for each of the republics. It also shows the percentage of GDP that was traded (average of exports and imports) in each republic, and the proportion of that which was traded with other republics rather than with the outside world (including the other members of the Council for Mutual Economic Assistance, or CMEA, consisting mainly of the Central European countries) in 1988. It can be seen that Russia exported the *lowest* proportion of GDP to other republics—some 13 percent of output—and the *highest* proportion to the outside world, although this was

TABLE A.1 Population, area, output, and trade in the republics of the former Soviet Union

Republic	Population (1990)		Area as a percentage of Soviet total	NMP as a percentage of Soviet total (1990)	Per capita income as a percentage of Soviet average (1988)	Total trade as a percentage of GDP (1988)	Interrepublic trade (1988)	
	Millions	As a percentage of Soviet total					As a percentage of total trade	As a percentage of GDP
Russia	148.0	51.3	76.2	61.2	110	22	58	13
Ukraine	51.8	17.9	2.7	16.2	96	34	79	27
Uzbekistan	20.3	7.0	2.0	3.2	62	40	86	34
Kazakhstan	16.7	5.8	12.1	4.6	93	34	86	29
Belarus	10.3	3.6	0.9	4.0	102	51	86	44
Azerbaijan	7.1	2.5	0.4	1.5	71	42	86	36
Georgia	5.5	1.9	0.3	1.5	108	44	87	38
Tajikistan	5.2	1.8	0.6	0.8	54	42	86	36
Kyrghyzstan	4.4	1.5	0.9	0.8	72	45	87	39
Moldova	4.4	1.5	0.2	1.3	84	53	88	47
Lithuania	3.7	1.3	0.3	1.4	114	55	87	48
Turkmenistan	3.6	1.2	2.2	0.7	71	39	89	35
Armenia	3.3	1.1	0.1	0.9	86	55	89	49
Latvia	2.7	0.9	0.3	1.2	123	55	87	48
Estonia	1.6	0.6	0.2	0.7	133	64	85	54

NMP = net material product.

Sources: International Monetary Fund (IMF), World Bank. Organization for Economic Cooperation and Development, and European Bank for Reconstruction and Development. 1991. *A Study of the Soviet Economy,* volume 1, 206–31 (Paris: published jointly); and International Monetary Fund. 1992. *Economic Review: Common Issues and Interrepublic Relations in the Former USSR,* 37, 42 (Washington: IMF). Data reprinted with permission

still a modest 9 percent. The Soviet republics traded extensively among themselves but very little with the outside world, which was precisely what the planners had intended given their aim of creating a self-sufficient economy organized as a single unit.

According to the paper presented to the conference by Sergei Vasiliev, the CIS can be divided into two main zones plus the peripheral region of Central Asia. One zone includes northern and central Russia, the Urals, Siberia, and the Far East: this region is "huge and ethnically polka-dotted . . . overstresses heavy industry and starves the almost depopulated agrarian sector." The other "includes Belarus, Ukraine, Moldova, Novorussia (the area just north of the Caucasus, including the cities of Rostov, Krasnodar, and Stavropol), the Caucasus itself, and Kazakhstan. . . . [I]ts ethnically mixed populations have been actively engaged in grass-roots entrepreneurial activity . . . [and are] major manufacturers of consumer goods . . . [with] a relatively strong agricultural sector." Thus Vasiliev places most of Russia in the zone with the characteristic planners' ailments of too much heavy industry and too little entrepreneurial initiative, and groups only a southern tier with the other non-Islamic republics with more promising economic attributes.

Russians dominated the key decision-making positions in the union government. This is why it is natural to regard the Soviet Union as a prolongation of the life of the Russian Empire beyond its natural term. But when democracy triumphed, Russia made no effort to hold the Soviet Union together. This surprised many Western observers, who had assumed that Russia would defend the territorial integrity of the Soviet Union with the same sort of tenacity that drove, say, Nigeria or Sudan to defeat attempts at secession. In fact many—although surely not all—Russians seem to have accepted rather easily that the ambition to become a "normal country" meant the ending of empire just as much as the adoption of democracy and a market economy, and so far it is this group that seems to have the upper hand in Russian policymaking. But the breakup of the Soviet Union still left Russia itself with ethnic minorities comprising some 18 percent of its population; some of these were organized in 16 autonomous republics, 5 autonomous oblasts, and 10 autonomous okrugs. The two most explosive regions currently appear to be Tatarstan (in the very heart of Russia east of Gorky) and Chechen-Ingush (on the northern slopes of the Caucasus range).

In November 1991 Russian President Boris Yeltsin appointed Yegor Gaidar to head the Russian economic team as First Deputy Prime Minister. Gaidar is only 35 years old, but he quickly established a formidable reputation as a dedicated reformer and a competent techno- crat with a lot of political horse sense. The Gaidar team immediately started to plan a "big bang" package of simultaneous radical economic reforms to try and make up some of the time that had been lost on endless shilly-shallying during the years of perestroika. One can argue that they had little option: goods had become almost totally unavailable on the shelves, which undermined both the incentive to work and that to repatriate dollars earned from exporting. The economy was bound to continue running down as long as this situation persisted, so even if the initial reaction to shock treatment was as negative as it had been in Poland and Czechoslovakia, it was better to get it over with and start to create the conditions under which some recovery might begin to be conceivable.

Most prices were liberalized on 2 January 1992, after less than eight weeks of preparation.[1] State orders were abolished. The program also included a bold attempt to establish fiscal discipline. The most important element consisted of the elimination of subsidies that had amounted to as much as 10 percent of GDP. This was backed by a drastic cut in military procurement and a large increase in taxes, notably in the rate and coverage of the value-added tax (VAT).[2] The economic team also hoped that monetary policy would be tightened sharply, but this was the responsibility of a central bank that, responding to Western advice to make it independent, reported to the populist-minded parliament rather than to the executive. In the event it seems that the governor of

---

1. Exceptions were energy, housing, utilities, and a few "socially necessary goods" like bread, milk, and vodka.

2. This tax, according to some accounts, is so far largely a sales tax. The rate was initially increased from 5 percent to 28 percent, but in February 1992, under pressure from the parliament, it was reduced to 15 percent for some goods. Sergey Alexashenko estimates (in a personal communication to the author) that the VAT yielded revenues of 6.9 percent of GNP in the first quarter of 1992, as against a yield of the turnover tax that it replaced of about 12 percent of GNP in 1990 and 7.7 percent of GNP in 1991 (when the VAT also yielded 1.1 percent of GNP).

the central bank, Georgy Matyukhin,[3] found it difficult to break out of the populist easy-credit stance developed in 1991 while seeking to undermine the position of the union Gosbank. There has not so far been much sign of the imposition of hard budget constraints.

The initial results of the Gaidar team's program were mixed. Some, but by no means all, goods did reappear on shop shelves in early 1992, but at the cost of extremely high inflation: 245 percent in January, 38 percent in February, 31 percent in March, and 20 percent in April (according to figures supplied by Sergey Alexashenko). Purchases fell drastically, with households drawing on the stocks that they had built up during the preceding months and years. Industrial production is reported to have fallen by a further 15 percent in the first quarter of 1992 from the already-depressed level of late 1991, and food production by substantially more. There were reports of perishable goods being allowed to rot on the shelves because no one who knew about it had the authority or the initiative to cut prices. The budget deficit contracted sharply, as did monetary expansion, but interenterprise credits exploded. The ruble recovered a little from its hyperdepreciated rate, presumably encouraged by the extreme shortage of cash rubles.

Despite the disappointments of some of the initial reactions to reform, the intention of the government is to press on. Small privatization continues to be a weak point, with only 0.7 percent of small enterprises privatized in the first quarter of 1992 and the process still being impeded by local governments, many of which are still controlled by the nomenklatura. The prices of most of the "socially necessary goods" have already been decontrolled. Energy prices have been increased again (although not yet liberalized as had been intended, partly in response to pressure from other republics), which should permit a further strengthening of the fiscal situation as well as create an incentive to economize on energy so as to release supplies for export. It was also announced shortly after the conference that Russia plans to make the ruble convertible, in the sense of unifying the various exchange rates (other than a parallel rate for households), on 1 July 1992, and to peg the ruble some time thereafter.

---

3. Matyukhin resigned in early June 1992, just as this study went to press.

Russia's relations with the other new states could also be described as mixed. Russia is so much larger than any of them that the role of hegemon seems natural. Moreover, Russia views most of the other states as lagging in the reform process, and feels it has a responsibility to lay down rules to counteract the temptation of other republics to free ride at the cost of undermining reform. Thus in November 1991 Russia already announced that it would restrict the supply of cash rubles to the other republics to no larger a proportionate increase than Russia itself was receiving. In January 1992 it took the further step of starting to redirect interrepublic payments through correspondent accounts, as explained in section 3 of this study. This will in due course give Russia a tool that it can use to avoid accepting bank-deposit rubles created in the other states.

Vasiliev's conference paper explains that in late 1991 the Russian government came under strong pressure from the other republics to sign barter agreements that would preserve compulsory deliveries. The Russian Ministry of Trade was sufficiently unreconstructed to be happy to agree, and a series of such agreements were signed. One problem with these agreements is that they are too poorly specified to function smoothly. Even where deliveries are designated in physical terms, there are no delivery dates specified. Furthermore, some goods are defined in value (i.e., ruble) terms, which is obviously inadequate in an environment verging on hyperinflation. The second and more fundamental problem with the barter agreements is that Russia has abolished the mechanism of state orders that in principle is needed to ensure that the agreements are fulfilled. Hence it is no great surprise to find Vasiliev reporting that "early 1992 saw an alarming slump in interrepublic goods turnover and [a] further decline in production."

Ukraine

Although it comprises less than 3 percent of the land surface of the former Soviet Union (which still makes it bigger than France), Ukraine is the second-largest successor state in terms of population (52 million people, or 18 percent of the total), GDP, and both industrial and agricultural production. GDP per capita was slightly below the average for the

Soviet Union in 1988. Industry contained a disproportionate share of the dinosaurs of Soviet heavy industry, but Ukraine's agricultural land includes some of the richest in Europe. Energy supplies are largely restricted to low-productivity coal mines, with a modest level of oil and gas production inadequate to supply more than a fraction of the domestic market.

Few Westerners were conscious of the existence of any widespread or intense national feeling in Ukraine until recently. In fact, however, the Communist old guard seemed to find it rather easy to swap their traditional garb for a very popular cloak of nationalism. Unlike in Russia, where the present government consists of reformers who had opposed the previous regime (or at least kept aloof from it), most of the Ukrainian government consists of people who served, apparently contentedly, during the Soviet regime. The government nonetheless declares itself committed to political democracy and the establishment of a market economy, as well as full national independence.

It has certainly displayed considerable zeal in the latter quest. It won a referendum in favor of independence in December 1991, even succeeding in gaining a majority of the votes among the substantial minority of ethnic Russians. Ukraine was a founder-member of the CIS, but once this had served its function of facilitating the dissolution of the Soviet Union, Ukrainian efforts appeared to turn to restraining— some might say emasculating—any effective CIS role. Thus it appeared that, at the initial CIS meetings in December 1991, Ukraine had agreed to a moratorium on the introduction of separate currencies at least until the end of 1992; yet it proceeded to introduce coupons to supplement rubles in January 1992 and to make plans for the introduction of a full-fledged currency, the hryvnia, in the course of the year. There have also been a series of squabbles with Russia about the disposition of military assets, notably the Black Sea fleet, as a result of Ukraine's quest to establish itself as a significant military power. It is not clear that Ukraine will even remain a member of the CIS much longer.

Although Ukraine has committed itself to building a market economy, it has not been a pioneer in introducing reforms. It had little option but to follow Russia in increasing many prices when Russia liberalized at the start of 1992, to avoid goods being bid away despite the imperfections of arbitrage, but it has not abolished state orders and it liberalized less than

70 percent of consumer-goods prices. Unfortunately the conference did not hear a paper on Ukraine that would have provided details on what has already happened or what is planned.[4]

We did, however, receive a report from Daniel Gros of the Centre for European Policy Studies, who had come directly from Kiev, that it is estimated that Ukrainian trade with the other former republics had declined by some 40 percent from the comparable period of 1991. Once again, therefore, such evidence as exists points to a sharp fall in intratrade among the former Soviet republics.

Moldova

Moldova is a small, landlocked republic on the western edge of the former Soviet Union, sharing borders with Ukraine and Romania. The bulk of the population is ethnically akin to the Romanians, but there is also a sizable Slavic (Ukrainian and Russian) minority concentrated in the northeastern part of the state. The majority wanted independence and is believed to be sympathetic to the possibility of an ultimate union with Romania, while at least the Russian part of the minority would have preferred to stick with Russia. Production is predominantly agricultural, and per capita income was the lowest in the non-Islamic republics. Moldova has announced its intention of introducing a separate currency in the course of 1992.

Belarus

Belarus is another landlocked country on what used to be the western border of the Soviet Union. It is comparable in size to several of the other countries of Eastern Europe, with roughly the population of Hungary and the area of Romania, although some 20 percent of its

---

4. A paper had been commissioned from Oleh Havrylyshyn, but shortly before the conference took place he was appointed Deputy Minister of Finance, and his participation in the conference was crowded out.

territory is no longer safely habitable as a consequence of the Chernobyl disaster just over the border in Ukraine. Belarus is relatively homogeneous in ethnic terms, with 80 percent of the population being Belarussian and two-thirds of the remainder being the closely related Russians. There was not much of an indigenous nationalist movement prior to independence, but people seem to have been happy enough to take political independence when it was offered to them. The present government remains with many of the same personnel as in the last years of Communist rule.

Belarus gained from the economic structure created by the Soviet planners, who built a diversified and extensive industrial base with many assembly industries in what had formerly been a predominantly agricultural area without the advantage of particularly fertile soils. Despite the absence of a favorable resource base, per capita income had risen in relative terms to a level marginally above the Soviet average, as the lack of resources was compensated by a high level of skills (one worker in eight has received a higher education). Another consequence of its industrial development was that Belarus traded very extensively with other Soviet republics: as shown in table A.1, over 50 percent of GDP was exported, some 86 percent of it to other republics. These figures would suggest that Belarus is particularly vulnerable to a breakdown in intratrade among the former Soviet republics.

So far economic collapse seems to have proceeded less far than in Russia. The conference paper on Belarus by Stanislav Bogdankiewicz, who is now Chairman of the National Bank of Belarus (the central bank), reports that GNP is estimated to have fallen by less than 2 percent in 1991.[5] The state budget was reported to be in surplus in 1991 (although presumably this does not include as expenditure the sum that the union government thought it should have received but that Belarus did not pay), and the deficit expected in 1992 remains moderate (the government is prohibited by law from running a deficit exceeding 6 percent of expenditure).

---

5. However, there is some question as to whether the newly created statistical services of the republics may not be overoptimistic. Goskomstat, the old and more qualified Soviet statistical service, estimated the decline of Soviet GNP in 1991 at 17 percent, yet none of the republics report a decline greater than 9 percent!

Belarus only began planning an independent liberalization program in December 1990, but in the following 12 months the legislature passed 43 laws, with a further batch approved in March 1992. Small privatization has started on a modest scale, and about 8 percent of output is now produced in the private sector. Prices were largely decontrolled, except for a basket of rationed consumer necessities, after Russia liberalized in January 1992. Bogdankiewicz reports that "the system of rationing of material resources has been dismantled, yet the alternative market mechanisms still do not function properly." However, he also tells us there are now 20 commercial exchanges doing business worth some 15 billion rubles per month, suggesting that one of the most promising market mechanisms is in fact developing.

Belarus is currently in a difficult intermediate situation as regards its ability to conduct a stabilization policy. It clearly needs to worry about its own situation, if only because of the limited overdraft rights imposed on its correspondent account at the Russian central bank. But at the same time its links with its big neighbor are so close that it would be very difficult to stabilize prices unless Russia does too, even with a separate currency, although that would have to be attempted if Russia fails to stabilize. The obvious solution is monetary cooperation, involving an agreed policy of credit creation, continued use of a common currency, and an agreed policy on ruble convertibility. But Bogdankiewicz complained bitterly at the conference that Russia's insistence on laying down policy unilaterally, and requiring any state that wished to continue using the ruble to fall into line, was making it impossible to contemplate continuing to use the ruble indefinitely. The Reuters news service reported after the conference that, to alleviate cash shortages, Belarus will introduce its own ruble to circulate in parallel with the Russian ruble on 1 July 1992. Unless Russia succeeds in stabilizing prices and Belarus can achieve some sharing of power, it would seem highly likely that it will introduce a completely separate national currency in due course.

The Baltic States

Although any Estonian, Latvian, or Lithuanian is acutely conscious of the differences among the three countries, they have sufficient similarities from the standpoint of this study to make it convenient to treat them together. In the first place, all three desire to reestablish their historic links, based on ethnic origin, language, culture, and religion, with European neighbors to the north or west (Estonia with Finland, Latvia with the other Scandinavian countries, and Lithuania with Germany), and to break their enforced ties to their Slavic neighbors to the east or south. Accordingly, all three refused to join the CIS, despite the terms-of-trade cost (higher energy prices) that they knew would result. Second, all three are of roughly similar size: in area they are comparable to the smaller European countries like Austria or Hungary, but their populations are substantially less (ranging from 1.6 million in Estonia to 3.7 million in Lithuania). The Baltic republics were three of the five smallest, in terms of population, in the Soviet Union. Third, they had the highest per capita incomes in the former Soviet Union, despite a modest natural resource base, but were nonetheless acutely conscious of how far they had fallen behind their European peers during the period of Soviet rule. Fourth, they have more recent memories of markets than elsewhere, plus recollections of prewar democracy.

The three Baltic states all had reasonably diversified industrial sectors and had maintained a relatively substantial base in agriculture and forestry. Their economies were nonetheless deeply integrated with the rest of the Soviet Union: all three exported to other republics close to 50 percent of GDP. They also possessed important transit routes for the foreign trade of Russia, a role given particular importance by the fact that Russia's own Baltic ports are usually icebound in winter.

Eagerness to launch economic reform has not spared the Baltics from the economic collapse that afflicted the rest of the Soviet Union. Inna Shteinbuka, the Latvian author of the conference paper on the Baltic states, reports that the industrial production of state enterprises fell in 1991 by 9 percent in Estonia, by 2 percent in Latvia, and by 1 percent in Lithuania. Comparing January 1992 with the same month a year earlier, the decline was over 25 percent in Latvia (the only country for which she had figures). Shteinbuka claims that the fall in production is in part a consequence of the decline in trade with the rest of the former Soviet Union, and asserts that "The Baltic republics do not get the commodities allocated from the centralized union funds."

The Baltic countries did conclude trade agreements with most members of the CIS in late 1991. These agreements were based on world market prices and ruble clearing, but it is not clear that Russia is in any position to stand by their terms since centralized supply sources no longer exist. The perception in the Baltics is nonetheless that they are not getting the goods needed to keep their economies producing, *inter alia* because of deliberate action by the Russian government (Shteinbuka even speaks of a Russian economic blockade). Shteinbuka relates that in February 1992 "about 100 Lithuanian enterprises could not function at full capacity for lack of deliveries from the CIS. Twenty thousand people had to stop work . . . because of shortage of raw materials. . . . [D]elivery of fuel to Estonia from the CIS was forecast to stop completely. Blocking of supplies and uncertainty about the development of relations with the CIS . . . seem to be the major factors behind the economic depression in the Baltic countries."

Prices were liberalized gradually in the Baltic states in the course of 1991, with Estonia in the lead. The process of price liberalization was largely concluded early in 1992, and state orders were abolished. Inflation appears to be as much out of hand as in Russia, which is hardly surprising as long as they more or less share a currency. The Baltics are seeking to introduce their own currencies at the earliest possible opportunity,[6] although Shteinbuka cautions that it would be silly to do this until the preconditions that may make stabilization possible have been satisfied, and she doubts whether that is conceivable in 1992. She also expresses the view that it would be sensible for the Baltic countries to replace the ruble with a joint currency rather than three separate ones, but she declares that this has been ruled out by emotional considerations, and therefore she did not judge it worthwhile to develop the case for a common currency in her paper.

Shteinbuka argues that the high degree of integration of the Baltic economies with those of the CIS would suggest maintaining economic ties with the eastern republics during a transition period, while trade is gradually reoriented toward the world market—hopefully assisted by a flow of inward direct investment. Such investment, primarily from Finland, is already playing a significant role in Estonia through the many joint ventures operating there.

---

6. Estonia announced after the conference that it would introduce its currency in June 1992.

Armenia

Armenia is an ancient nation on the southern border of the old Soviet Union, in the Caucasus. The author of the conference paper on Armenia, Suren Karapetyan, asserts that only Nepal and Lesotho have more hopeless geographical locations, for Armenia is "a small, mountainous country situated in the depth of the continent, without access to the sea or other waterways." He might have added that three of the four countries with which it shares a border are Islamic, whereas Armenia has been Christian for 1,700 years. Armenia is in active conflict with its eastern neighbor Azerbaijan over the Nagorno-Karabakh province, and has therefore been subjected to intermittent blockade of most goods, including most fuel since November 1991; to the south, fundamentalist Iran does not try to hide the fact that its sympathies lie with Azerbaijan; only Armenia's historical enemy, Turkey, behaves as a moderately good neighbor.[7] Armenia's only non-Islamic neighbor, Georgia, lies over a mountain range penetrated only by a single-track railway that constitutes Armenia's sole link with the rest of the former Soviet Union when the Azerbaijani blockade is enforced. Even that railway, which in the best of times can carry only a quarter of Armenia's trade, is periodically put out of commission by sabotage directed against the Georgian government, which in any event does not go out of its way to ensure ready transit. It is not clear that Nepal's situation is worse.

Armenia's current problems are compounded by two other tragedies and an attempt to avert a third. The devastating 1988 earthquake destroyed something like a third of the country's capital stock, a loss that has still not been made good. Meanwhile deportations of thousands of persons from Azerbaijan to Armenia and vice versa have followed the escalation of their conflict over Nagorno-Karabakh. The tragedy that has not happened is a nuclear disaster, but the cost of ensuring that it does not is the loss of over a third of the country's potential output

---

7. It would be difficult to blame Armenians for hesitating to rely on this attitude persisting indefinitely, but Karapetyan argues that Turkey's commitment to democratic values and the West is now firm enough to make it sensible for Armenians to exploit the opportunities of developing transit routes through Turkey.

of electricity. Karapetyan argues that the uncertain gain of closing down the plant just because it lies in an earthquake zone is not worth the certain cost. The rest of us may be torn between relief that the Armenian government has not endorsed his judgment, and dismay at the sacrifices that the Armenian people are making in reducing the risks the whole world would face.

Armenia was not only the smallest of the Soviet republics in area (comparable to Belgium), but the smallest in population outside the Baltics as well, with some 3.3 million people. Per capita income was below the Soviet mean. The republic produced primarily consumer goods and skill-intensive products for the Soviet market, to which it exported about 50 percent of its GDP. It imported much of its foodstuffs and most of its fossil fuels, which left it very vulnerable to any breakdown in intratrade, including disruptions in the transportation system. (Armenia's only gas pipeline runs through Azerbaijan, although an oil pipeline is being laid through Georgia.) Many of the new states have a strong interest in securing guaranteed rights of transit, but nowhere is that interest stronger than in Armenia.

According to Karapetyan, output fell by some 14 percent in 1990 and a further 16 percent in 1991. The decline in 1992 will presumably be even more severe, since a lack of fuel closed down virtually everything in the early months of the year. Industrial production is reported to have fallen by 85 percent from the 1991 level. Living standards have clearly fallen catastrophically, although no statistical measure of the depth of the catastrophe seems available.

Armenians have long had a reputation for entrepreneurship, which may help explain why Armenia embarked on economic reform early, after anti-Communists were elected to office already in April 1990. The first land reform[8] in the Soviet Union took place not in the Baltic states but in Armenia, where 80 percent of the land had already been privatized in 1991, helping produce a 15 percent increase in agricultural output that year. By the summer of 1991 the government was even introducing

8. In the ex-Soviet context this phrase means the restoration of private ownership of land.

a private sector into health and education. But the benefits one might have expected from economic reform have been swamped by the problems that have arisen from the lack of inputs, notably of imported energy supplies.

Armenian attitudes to Soviet disintegration are in some respects parallel to those of Belarus, but even more pronounced. That is, despite the shortcomings of the Soviet state, it had the overwhelming virtue in Armenian eyes of providing some restraint on the actions of their hostile Azerbaijani neighbors. Karapetyan views with dismay the destruction of the union government by what he regards as power-hungry Russian leaders. The CIS was doomed to be ineffective from the start. The last thing Armenia needed was independence from Russia, but it has no alternative. It has to try and survive on its own. And its best hope in doing so lies in burying the historical hatchet with Turkey. (It is not clear whether Karapetyan's views on the latter topic are shared by the Armenian government.)

If it turns out that Karapetyan is too pessimistic about the CIS eventually emerging as an effective instrument of economic cooperation, presumably Armenia will be among the states that would welcome the chance to renew economic integration. Otherwise it will be interesting to see whether the republic turns to Turkey as he urges.

Azerbaijan

Armenia's neighbor and adversary in Nagorno-Karabakh feels just as passionately that it has been wronged in that dispute, and specifically that Armenia is using force to grab territory to which it has no legitimate claim. But while the conflict dominates Azerbaijan's political life to an equal degree, its strategic vulnerability is clearly less than Armenia's. It continued to be governed by former Communists at the time of the conference, but military disaster in the conflict with Armenia spawned a popular uprising the following month that established the Azerbaijani Popular Front (reportedly a broad coalition of nationalist non-Communists) in government.

Azerbaijan is the largest of the three Caucasian states in terms of both area and population, with just over 7 million inhabitants in an area roughly the size of Austria. Its per capita income was distinctly lower than Armenia's and comparable with that in the other Muslim republics. This is despite the fact that at the turn of the century something like half the world's oil came from what is now Azerbaijan, and that on the basis of this business it built up specialized engineering industries that still supply oil-drilling equipment to fields throughout what used to be the Soviet Union. Azerbaijan's degree of industrialization is so much greater than that in Central Asia that it is surprising to find an income level comparable with that in Kyrghyzstan and Turkmenistan. As recently as 1960 living standards were close to the average for the Soviet Union.

Industry in Azerbaijan is primarily heavy. Although Azerbaijan exported a substantial proportion (about 35 percent) of its GDP to other republics under the Soviet regime, this proportion was somewhat less than in most of the other small republics.

According to Korkhmaz Imanov, who contributed the conference paper on Azerbaijan, there was only a marginal fall in output in Azerbaijan in 1991. Whether this will remain true in 1992, especially as it seems that the intratrade of Azerbaijan is subject to erosion from the same forces as those operating elsewhere, appears doubtful. Failures to deliver in accordance with the terms of agreed barter contracts, especially by Ukraine, are already reported to have led to a sharp worsening in the consumer market.

Azerbaijan was a reluctant reformer under the previous government, and the process of launching a private sector via leasing and the establishment of cooperatives is still very limited. Presumably that will change under the new regime.

Georgia

The third of the new Caucasian states, Georgia, has an area similar to that of the Irish Republic and a substantially larger population, some 5.5 million. It traces its historical origins back to the sixth century B.C., and Georgians adopted Christianity as early as the fourth century A.D. But apart from a brief interlude in 1918-21, Georgia was effectively ruled by Russia from the beginning of the nineteenth century until the breakup of the Soviet Union.

Georgia is also a mountainous country, but it receives abundant rainfall and has rich agricultural potential as well as extensive hydropower resources. The planners insisted on Georgia having its quota of polluting industries, which imported materials and parts from the north and exported most of the output back there. It nevertheless remained famous for its agricultural produce, its cooking, and its wine, which were all recognized to be the finest in the Soviet Union. It was in such goods that Georgia had a positive balance of trade.

Georgia's emancipation from Communist rule proved to be the most traumatic so far witnessed in the former Soviet Union. The first elections were won by President Zviad Gamsakhurdia, but he quickly revealed himself to be a paranoid tyrant who proceeded to isolate Georgia from both the rest of the former Soviet Union and the West. His overthrow in early 1992 involved brutal and destructive warfare in the center of the capital, Tbilisi. In the meantime the economy spiraled into chaos and living standards declined drastically, according to David Onoprishvili, the author of the conference paper on Georgia.

Georgia until very recently had the highest per capita income of the three Caucasian republics. It was comfortably above the Soviet average in 1988, and almost as high as that of Russia. But Onoprishvili reports that this had already changed for the worse by 1990, when per capita income was estimated to be 7 percent below the Soviet average, while in 1991 national income fell a further 25 percent. Georgia exported about 38 percent of its GDP to the rest of the Soviet Union.

Economic reform did not start until the ouster of President Gamsakhurdia, whose tastes favored centralized state capitalism rather than the market economy. During his tenure the budget deficit got completely out of hand, reaching 50 percent of expenditure in 1991. The initial emphasis of the new government was, however, not on restoring fiscal discipline but on starting privatization. Dwellings were given to their occupants, and plots of arable land were given to tenants (subject to their working the land for at least two years prior to selling it). It was intended that land reform should be completed before sowing started in 1992. Privatization of small enterprises—trade, catering, woodworking, construction materials, light industry, and food processing—is also proceeding apace, with an expectation that it will raise some 11 billion rubles in 1992 and more in the future. Only the fate of the large manufacturing enterprises remains to be decided.

Onoprishvili discusses in his paper the merits of Georgia joining the CIS. He argues that membership would bring some very important material advantages: the prospect of reviving trade links, and thereby combating the current recession; the opportunity to sell the industrial products that the planners had resolved should be produced in Georgia; the chance of attracting investments in rubles (although the currency question is surely not as important a determinant of foreign investment as security of property rights); and the hope of being able to buy energy in larger quantities, and/or at lower prices, for rubles.

Nevertheless, he also sees severe disadvantages in Georgian membership. Once again one encounters the fear of Russian domination, specifically a fear that it would be necessary to follow Russia's lead in fiscal and monetary policy. Onoprishvili also expresses the fear that membership would tend to petrify the existing productive structure and impede the chance of the country finding its own special niche from which it can exploit its geopolitical situation in the wider world. The continued use of the ruble would be convenient, but he suggests that controversies over its management between Russia and Ukraine, and the shortage of cash rubles, mean that it would be prudent to invest in an independent currency.

Finally, Onoprishvili points to political considerations. The Georgian people voted overwhelmingly for independence, and they are skeptical about the CIS. Russia has twice in the past violated Georgia's independence. Costly as it may be initially for Georgia to seek independent integration into the world economy and a separate currency, that would clearly be Onoprishvili's choice. He sees that as quite compatible with functional cooperation with the CIS on specific projects, for example in the environmental field, and with bilateral agreements with the member states, including payments agreements.

Kazakhstan

Kazakhstan is the second-largest of the new states by area, comprising some 12 percent of the territory of the former Soviet Union. Its population of near 17 million is, however, only the fourth-largest.

The northern part of the country is populated mainly by Russians, who comprise nearly 40 percent of the republic's population and are almost as numerous as Kazakhs. Many of the Russian immigrants were brought to Kazakhstan in the 1960s in pursuit of Nikita Khrushchev's dream of solving the Soviet Union's perennial agricultural shortages by cultivating the "virgin lands."

Kazakhstan has rich natural resources, including hydrocarbons and minerals as well as agricultural land, and accordingly its place in the socialist division of labor was primarily to supply raw materials. Perhaps surprisingly in view of this role, the percentage of NMP exported to the other republics was under 30 percent.[9] Kazakhstan had a per capita income somewhat below the Soviet average, but well above that in the neighboring Islamic states in Central Asia.

Although the country has remained under the firm political control of President Nursultan Nazarbayev throughout the period of transition to date, it has encountered many of the same economic problems as its large neighbor to the north: declining production (a measured fall of about 10 percent in 1991, including a smaller but nonetheless damaging fall in energy output) and an out-of-control budget deficit. Beisenbay Izteleuov, the author of the conference paper on Kazakhstan, argues that a large part of the blame for the cut in output lies with the failure of other republics to deliver the quantities specified in the interrepublic

---

9. However, the measured ratio of exports to NMP was lowered by the systematic underpricing of everything that Kazakhstan sold under the planners' prices.

barter deals that Kazakhstan had negotiated (deals whose terms Kazakhstan largely continued to fulfill on the export side). Imports of consumer goods, on which the state is exceptionally dependent to satisfy the internal market because of the predominance of extractive industry, have fallen sharply.

Izteleuov anticipates a dramatic worsening in the situation in the course of 1992, with unemployment rising from a scant 4,000 to some 1.7 million. Once again, a dominant cause is the lack of needed inputs from the other states. In 1992 it is not just a failure of other republics to deliver what they had promised to supply, but in many cases it has proved impossible even to extract promises to deliver. Izteleuov estimates that the national income produced in Kazakhstan decreased by about 30 percent in the first two months of 1992 as against a year earlier.

Kazakhstan was not a pioneer in introducing the market economy. It has tended to follow Russia reluctantly, for example in liberalizing prices and introducing a "value-added tax" in January. The VAT yielded little revenue, at least at first, because no preparations had been made for its introduction. Despite this, the 1992 budget deficit is projected to be only 2.6 percent of GNP, thanks to radical economies in expenditure, including large cuts in subsidies to loss-making enterprises and reductions in administrative expenditure.

Small privatization is "developing rapidly" according to Izteleuov, although land is still only leased, not sold. A diversity of methods, including both sale and some form of free distribution, are being planned to privatize large enterprises in due course. Despite the progress with privatization, Izteleuov complains that enterprises are still indifferent to market signals. But one encouraging development announced after the conference was that the massive deal whereby Chevron would develop a new oil field in Kazakhstan had finally been signed.

The country shows no enthusiasm for independence. The president resented the failure of the three large Slavic states to invite him to participate in the initial meetings that founded the CIS at Brest last December, and he quickly demanded the right to join in. Since then Kazakhstan's efforts have been directed toward strengthening the CIS, and Izteleuov's paper complains about the disruption being caused by arbitrary and unilateral decisions that are tearing apart the integrated economy that, for better or for worse, had been created on the territory of the Soviet Union. Kazakhstan would prefer a coordinated monetary and credit policy and a single money rather than monetary independence.

Izteleuov appears to retain little hope that the CIS will develop into an effective mechanism of economic coordination, but he speculates that a more limited grouping consisting of Russia, Belarus, Kazakhstan, and perhaps Kyrghyzstan might yet get together to found a new economic union. He envisages that such a union would provide for the free movement of goods, services, capital, and labor, and coordinate policy with regard to finance, money, credit, taxes, prices, and social policy.

Central Asia

Like the Baltic states, the four new states in Central Asia—or, as the Russians call it, Middle Asia—think of themselves as very different from one another. And so they are, in a number of ways. Yet they have enough in common for it to be convenient to discuss the four together.

In the first place, all four are Islamic countries with historically high population growth rates. Second, they were among the five poorest republics in the old Soviet Union, with Azerbaijan rated as having only marginally lower per capita income than the richest of the four, Kyrghyzstan (sometimes referred to as Kirghizia). Third, they were all assigned the role of producing raw materials (primarily cotton, except in Kyrghyzstan) in the socialist division of labor: less than 30 percent of employment was in industry, and over 30 percent was in agriculture. Such industry as did exist was staffed primarily by the Russian minority rather than by the local population. Fourth, they all received substantial transfers of income through the fiscal system, which limited the dispersion in consumption standards among the 15 republics. (However, they were not large recipients of implicit subsidies through the internal price structure of the Soviet Union: on the contrary, three of the four—and especially Turkmenistan—were expected to benefit from improved terms of trade as a result of the shift to world prices.) Finally, all of them exported between 35 percent and 40 percent of their GDP to other republics.

Uzbekistan is the largest of the four, with a population of almost 21 million and an area of 2 percent of the former Soviet Union (larger than united Germany but smaller than France). It is run by the National Democratic Party, which is the reformed Communist Party. Its economy is dominated by the production of cotton, of which it produced over 60 percent of the Soviet total. Uzbekistan nonetheless produced less than 6 percent of Soviet cotton fabrics, a disparity resented in the republic as a vivid symbol of economic colonialism. Seeking to grow ever more cotton in an area with minimal rainfall, the planners diverted into irrigation virtually all the water that used to flow into the Aral Sea. The result is that this large, shallow saltwater lake has been drying up, and is already reduced to half its former area. Dry salt from the former seabed is blown by the winds, causing both human discomfort and ecological havoc. Perhaps only Chernobyl ranks as a greater catastrophe in the catalogue of ecological devastation bequeathed by the Soviet government.[10]

The second-largest of the four states in terms of population (5.4 million), although the smallest in area (about the size of England), is Tajikistan. This is the only republic where an avowedly Communist government was still in office when the Vienna conference was held in April 1992 (it was pushed out of office by a coalition of democratic and Islamic forces the following month). According to some accounts the Communist revolution was very simple here because the feudal chiefs simply signed up as commissars and life proceeded without much interruption. Tajikistan was the poorest of all the republics, with a per capita income little over half the union average. It is perched in the Himalaya mountains and shares borders with Afghanistan and China.

Kyrghyzstan is also a mountainous state, lying immediately to the north of Tajikistan, again sharing a border with China. Its 4.4 million people are reputed to be the best educated and most entrepreneurial of the region, and its government has the reputation of being the most

---

10. To be fair to the planners, they had intended to avoid the Aral's desiccation by reversing the course of several rivers that flow to the Arctic. Environmental concerns led to the abandonment of those grandiose plans in the early Gorbachev years. Whether the environment was a net beneficiary of that decision is not obvious to the casual observer.

democratic. Industry comprises a somewhat larger share of the economy, and the Russian minority a somewhat larger share of the population (over 20 percent rather than under 10 percent) than elsewhere in the region. These factors presumably explain why Kyrghyzstan has a somewhat higher per capita income than Uzbekistan despite a smaller resource base. The government is the only one of the four that gives the impression that it welcomes, rather than just tolerates, the switch to a market economy.

Turkmenistan is the largest of the four states in terms of area and the smallest in terms of population (3.7 million). It borders Iran (and Afghanistan) to the south, thus giving it the opportunity of developing trade links in that direction. Plans are already afoot to improve transport links—including the construction of pipelines—so as to be able to export to the world market. Turkmenistan has rich hydrocarbon resources (mainly natural gas), which already gave it a per capita income almost as high as Kyrghyzstan's in 1988 and made it a net energy exporter.

The dominant economic problem of the region has for some time been its growing dependence on income transfers from the union budget. According to Rustam Narzikulov, the author of the conference paper on the region, net domestic material product per person employed declined from 83 percent of the Soviet average in 1970, to 66 percent in 1979, and to a mere 51 percent in 1989. Consumption levels did not decline proportionately because of increasing transfers from the union budget. On the contrary, ownership per family of many consumer durables (including cars) was above the Soviet average, although the average family was of course much larger. The local peoples showed a preference for a quiet life, often refusing to take jobs in industry or construction because the additional pay was not judged to be worth the extra effort.

However, transfers had already stabilized in the second half of the 1980s. They have now disappeared as a result of the disintegration of the Soviet Union. In 1991 transfers made up about half of all budget revenues, hence a quarter or more of GDP, and were sufficient to keep the republics' budget deficits down to reasonable levels, between 5.5 percent and 7.5 percent of budget expenditure. Without the budgetary transfers those deficits would have been 58 percent of produced national income in Uzbekistan, 38 percent in Kyrghyzstan, and 35 percent in Tajikistan. The draft budget of Tajikistan for 1992 showed revenues of

3.6 billion rubles and expenditures of 7.6 billion rubles, with no sources to finance the deficit. In fact the necessity of imitating the Russian lead in liberalizing prices at the beginning of the year—or at least raising them, since in at least two states prices were refrozen within weeks—led to an unexpected improvement in the fiscal situation, but this is expected to be temporary (presumably because expenditures will in due course rise to overwhelm the increase in revenue).

The abrupt termination of transfers is paralleled by an organizational collapse in those sectors of the economy that had been integrated into the national economy of the Soviet Union, such as energy production, railways, and centrally supplied food. Three of the Central Asian states, the exception being Kyrghyzstan, have substantial trade deficits in foodstuffs.

Changes in Central Asia are, according to Narzikulov, likely to occur only as forced reactions to changes elsewhere. Given the opportunity of retaining an association with Russia or the CIS, and thus continuing to receive at least some part of the transfers to which they have become accustomed, the Central Asian states would jump at the chance. Past political declarations in favor of independence would not be a stumbling block.

Changes in the structure of ownership are likely to be slower than elsewhere in the former Soviet Union, in part because of the continuing tendency to regulate the activities of nonstate enterprises and the fear of potential owners, based on past experience, that they may be closed down. Indeed, the governments of three of the states, the exception again being Kyrghyzstan, would really prefer to retain a highly centralized system dominated by state property, as well as strong redistributive measures to equalize incomes. Privatization of small service sectors may occur, but privatization is unlikely to reach industry or agriculture. However, Narzikulov notes some possibly reluctant but nonetheless quite strong recent steps in Turkmenistan toward introducing a market economy, and other observers seem less pessimistic than he is about the strength of resistance to change in the region.

The dominant economic issue posed to the region by Soviet disintegration is the need for a classic adjustment program, with brutal cuts in consumption, in order to compensate for the loss of fiscal transfers from the union budget.

References

Brabant, Jozef M. van. 1991. "Convertibility in Eastern Europe Through a Payments Union." In John Williamson, ed., *Currency Convertibility in Eastern Europe*, 63–95. Washington: Institute for International Economics.

Camdessus, Michel. 1992. "IMF Could Provide $25–30 Billion to Republics of the Former Soviet Union." *IMF Survey* (27 April).

Collins, Susan M., and Dani Rodrik. 1991. *Eastern Europe and the Soviet Union in the World Economy*. POLICY ANALYSES IN INTERNATIONAL ECONOMICS 32. Washington: Institute for International Economics.

Gros, Daniel, and Berenize Dautrebande. 1992. "International Trade of Former Republics in the Long Run." Brussels: Centre for European Policy Studies (mimeographed).

De Long, J. B., and Barry Eichengreen. 1992. "The Marshall Plan: History's Most Successful Structural Adjustment Program." *CEPR Discussion Papers* 634. London: Centre for Economic Policy Research.

Goldberg, Linda. 1992. "Ruble Stabilization and Required Foreign-Exchange Market Reforms." New York: New York University (mimeographed).

Hanke, Steve H., and Kurt Schuler. 1991. "Currency Boards for Eastern Europe." *The Heritage Lectures* 355. Washington: The Heritage Foundation.

Havrylyshyn, Oleh, and John Williamson. 1991. *From Soviet disUnion to Eastern Economic Community?* POLICY ANALYSES IN INTERNATIONAL ECONOMICS 35. Washington: Institute for International Economics.

Institute of International Finance. 1992. *USSR/CIS Country Report*. Washington: Institute of International Finance (7 February).

International Monetary Fund. 1992. *Economic Review: Common Issues and Interrepublic Relations in the Former USSR*. Washington: International Monetary Fund.

International Monetary Fund, World Bank, Organization for Economic Cooperation and Development, and European Bank for Reconstruction and Development. 1990. *The Economy of the USSR: Summary and Recommendations*. Washington: published jointly.

International Monetary Fund, World Bank, Organization for Economic Cooperation and Development, and European Bank for Reconstruction and Development. 1991. *A Study of the Soviet Economy*. Paris: published jointly.

Kaplan, Jacob J., and Gunther Schleiminger. 1989. *The European Payments Union*. Oxford, England: Clarendon Press.

Nuti, D. Mario, and Jean Pisani-Ferry. 1992. "Post-Soviet Issues: Stabilization, Trade and Money." Paper presented at a conference on "Economic Consequences of the East," sponsored by the Centre for Economic Policy Research and the Deutsche Bundesbank, Frankfurt (April).

Portes, Richard. 1992. "Is There A Better Way?" *International Economic Insights* 3, no. 3 (May-June): 18–22.

Williamson, John. 1992a. "The Eastern Transition to a Market Economy: A Global Perspective." *Occasional Papers* 2. Centre for Economic Performance, London School of Economics.

Williamson, John. 1992b. *The Economic Consequences of Soviet Disintegration.* Washington: Institute for International Economics.

Wolf, Martin. 1992. "Russia Rolls the Dice of Reform." *Financial Times* (14 May).

Other Publications from the
Institute for International Economics

POLICY ANALYSES IN INTERNATIONAL ECONOMICS Series

1 **The Lending Policies of the International Monetary Fund**
John Williamson/*August 1982*
$8.00   ISBN paper 0-88132-000-5   72 pp.

2 **"Reciprocity": A New Approach to World Trade Policy?**
William R. Cline/*September 1982*
$8.00   ISBN paper 0-88132-001-3   41 pp.

3 **Trade Policy in the 1980s**
C. Fred Bergsten and William R. Cline/*November 1982*
(out of print)   ISBN paper 0-88132-002-1   84 pp.
Partially reproduced in the book *Trade Policy in the 1980s.*

4 **International Debt and the Stability of the World Economy**
William R. Cline/*September 1983*
$10.00   ISBN paper 0-88132-010-2   134 pp.

5 **The Exchange Rate System**
John Williamson/*September 1983, rev. June 1985*
(out of print)   ISBN paper 0-88132-034-X   61 pp.

6 **Economic Sanctions in Support of Foreign Policy Goals**
Gary Clyde Hufbauer and Jeffrey J. Schott/*October 1983*
$10.00   ISBN paper 0-88132-014-5   109 pp.

7 **A New SDR Allocation?**
John Williamson/*March 1984*
$10.00   ISBN paper 0-88132-028-5   61 pp.

8 **An International Standard for Monetary Stabilization**
Ronald I. McKinnon/*March 1984*
$10.00   ISBN paper 0-88132-018-8   108 pp.

9 **The Yen/Dollar Agreement: Liberalizing Japanese Capital Markets**
Jeffrey A. Frankel/*December 1984*
$10.00   ISBN paper 0-88132-035-8   86 pp.

10 **Bank Lending to Developing Countries: The Policy Alternatives**
C. Fred Bergsten, William R. Cline, and John Williamson/*April 1985*
$12.00   ISBN paper 0-88132-032-3   221 pp.

11 **Trading for Growth: The Next Round of Trade Negotiations**
Gary Clyde Hufbauer and Jeffrey J. Schott/*September 1985*
$10.00   ISBN paper 0-88132-033-1   109 pp.

12 **Financial Intermediation Beyond the Debt Crisis**
Donald R. Lessard and John Williamson/*September 1985*
$12.00   ISBN paper 0-88132-021-8   130 pp.

13 **The United States–Japan Economic Problem**
C. Fred Bergsten and William R. Cline/*October 1985, rev. January 1987*
$10.00   ISBN paper 0-88132-060-9   180 pp.

BOOKS

Economic Sanctions Reconsidered (in two volumes)
  Economic Sanctions Reconsidered: History and Current Policy
    (also sold separately, see below)
  Economic Sanctions Reconsidered: Supplemental Case Histories
Gary Clyde Hufbauer, Jeffrey J. Schott, and Kimberly Ann Elliott/
  1985, rev. December 1990

$65.00	ISBN cloth 0-88132-115-X	928 pp.
$45.00	ISBN paper 0-88132-105-2	928 pp.

Economic Sanctions Reconsidered: History and Current Policy
Gary Clyde Hufbauer, Jeffrey J. Schott, and Kimberly Ann Elliott/
  December 1990

$36.00	ISBN cloth 0-88132-136-2	288 pp.
$25.00	ISBN paper 0-88132-140-0	288 pp.

Pacific Basin Developing Countries: Prospects for the Future
Marcus Noland/*January 1991*

$29.95	ISBN cloth 0-88132-141-9	250 pp.
$19.95	ISBN paper 0-88132-081-1	250 pp.

Currency Convertibility in Eastern Europe
John Williamson, editor/*September 1991*

$39.95	ISBN cloth 0-88132-144-3	396 pp.
$28.95	ISBN paper 0-88132-128-1	396 pp.

Foreign Direct Investment in the United States
Edward M. Graham and Paul R. Krugman/*1989, rev. October 1991*

$19.00	ISBN paper 0-88132-139-7	200 pp.

International Adjustment and Financing: The Lessons of 1985–1991
C. Fred Bergsten, editor/*January 1992*

$34.95	ISBN cloth 0-88132-142-7	336 pp.
$24.95	ISBN paper 0-88132-112-5	336 pp.

North American Free Trade: Issues and Recommendations
Gary Clyde Hufbauer and Jeffrey J. Schott/*April 1992*

$42.50	ISBN cloth 0-88132-145-1	392 pp.
$25.00	ISBN paper 0-88132-120-6	392 pp.

American Trade Politics
I. M. Destler/*1986, rev. June 1992*

$35.00	ISBN cloth 0-88132-164-8	400 pp.
$20.00	ISBN paper 0-88132-188-5	400 pp.

Narrowing the U.S. Current Account Deficit: A Sectoral Assessment
Allen J. Lenz/*June 1992*

$40.00	ISBN cloth 0-88132-148-6	640 pp.
$25.00	ISBN paper 0-88132-103-6	640 pp.

The Economics of Global Warming
William R. Cline/*June 1992*

$40.00	ISBN cloth 0-88132-150-8	416 pp.
$20.00	ISBN paper 0-88132-132-X	416 pp.

SPECIAL REPORTS

FORTHCOMING